THE
NINE TRADES OF DUNDEE

ANNETTE M. SMITH

ABERTAY
HISTORICAL
SOCIETY

NUMBER 35
DUNDEE
1995

1. PLAQUE OF THE NINE TRADES, ST ANDREW'S CHURCH

(Spanphoto, Dundee)

ACKNOWLEDGEMENTS

First of all I must thank the Nine Trades for asking me to make this study of their history. I hope I have managed to pass on to the members of the Trades and the Abertay Historical Society the interest I have found in the subject.

One of the peculiarities of the relationship of the Nine Trades with its nine member societies is the independence of the individual incorporations. The General Fund Court might commission a history of all its parts but members do not necessarily need to cooperate. I must therefore express my gratitude to the clerks of the Bakers, Bonnetmakers, Cordiners, Fleshers, Hammermen, Tailors and Weavers, who went out of their way to make access to their records easy and convenient for me, to the extent of providing comfortable working space in busy lawyers' offices. This cannot always have been convenient for them and I appreciated their co-operation very much.

Many people have given help during my research. Mr Flett and Mr Cullen, Dundee District Archive and Record Centre, were towers of palaeographic strength. Mr R.N. Smart also gave invaluable assistance on occasion, and the late Professor I.B. Cowan and Dr J. Durkan solved a particularly knotty palaeographic problem for me. Members of the Trades have given me their time to provide information that could not be won from documents and here I must mention Dr O. Taylor Brown and Mr W. Philp, a master dyer.

I must particularly thank the Deacon-Conveners who have been in office while this work was in rather lengthier progress than any of us expected for their assistance, support and forbearance. Mr David Richardson was my first contact with the Nine Trades and his enthusiasm has been of great encouragement throughout. Mr David Goodfellow has very kindly lent me some of his own source material and has also helped me with some enquiries. Mr A. Scott has continued the pattern of encouragement shown by his two predecessors and I am very grateful to them all.

Mr C.J. Davey must also be thanked for his sympathetic editing. Last, but far from least, my husband's patience while I have been absorbed in the lives of all these other men must be given credit for making the venture possible at all.

This book was set in train by Deacon Convener David Richardson in 1990 and enthusiastically supported by his successor, Alastair Scott. I am delighted that it has come to fruition now, and that I can help launch it before a welcoming readership.

Prior to its arrival, the only proper reference book available to Tradesmen was A.J. Warden's *Burgh Laws*, published in 1872. A.J.W. was a prolific and enthusiastic amateur historian, not averse to a bit of guesswork, and much of his book is difficult to understand; speakers at Trades dinners had the unenviable task of trawling through its pages for material.

That has all changed with the appearance of this work. Dr Annette Smith is a professional historian, and one of the reasons that Convener Richardson approached her is that she wrote the history of Dundee's Three United Trades. She is the top authority on Dundee Trades matters.

Annette Smith is readable and accurate – and a pleasure to work with – and this book will be welcomed by present and future Tradesmen and historians.

The Nine Incorporated Trades of Dundee wish to congratulate and thank Dr Smith for undertaking the prolonged research and for the end product, which is this benchmark of a book.

Gordon Small
Deacon Convener
Christmas Eve 1994

CONTENTS

LIST OF ILLUSTRATIONS

ABBREVIATIONS

APS	Acts of the Parliaments of Scotland
DDARC	Dundee District Archive and Record Centre
DDL	Dundee District Library
NT	Nine Trades Archive
BLB	Baker Trade's Lockit Book
BMB	Baker Trade's Minute Book
BmT	Bonnetmaker Trade's Archive
BmTSB	Bonnetmaker Trade's Sederunt Book
BmTAB	Bonnetmaker Trade's Account Book
BmTMB	Bonnetmaker Trade's Minute Book
BmTLB	Bonnetmaker Trade's Lockit Book
CLB1	Cordiner Trade's Lockit Book, 1567–1774
CLB2	Cordiner Trade's Lockit Book, 1774– present
CSB	Cordiner Trade's Sederunt Book
DLB	Dyer Trade's Lockit Book
FLB	Flesher Trade's Lockit Book
FMB	Flesher Trade's Minute Book
GLB	Glover Trade's Lockit Book.
HMLB	Hammerman Trade's Lockit Book
TLB	Tailor Trade's Lockit Book
WLB	Weaver Trade's Lockit Book
WAB	Weaver Trade's Account Book
SHR	Scottish Historical Review

CHAPTER 1

Introduction

Since the sixteenth century at least various Trades of Dundee have worked together to advance the interests of their incorporations. There were nine who usually seemed to consult each other and gradually their co-operation became more formalised. They elected officers whose discipline they accepted and among themselves recognised an order of precedence. First came the Baxter Trade followed by the Cordiners, Glovers, originally Skinners, Tailors, Bonnetmakers, Fleshers, Hammermen, Brabeners and Waulkers. In 1693 the Litsters united with the Waulkers.

These are the Scottish names for the Trades but they now almost universally use the English form of their crafts; Bakers instead of Baxters, Shoemakers for Cordiners, Weavers instead of Brabeners or Websters, and Dyers for Litsters. The Waulkers were the fullers of cloth and the use of that name slowly disappeared after the union with the Dyers and was rarely used by the early nineteenth century. However, the list of Trades in order of seniority in the new constitution of the Nine Trades (1979) gives the older names first in two instances, the Cordiners and the Waulkers.

There were no recorded challenges to the accepted order of precedence until just after the two smallest Trades, the Dyers and Waulkers, united. Dundee's Head Court was asked in 1695 to change the ancient order of precedence. It seems to have been the new united society which initiated the attempt to change the ranking, probably believing that their larger numbers now deserved a higher place among their fellows. Not surprisingly the request was not successful. Quite apart from the lack of enthusiasm for any alteration to established order among Scottish burgh authorities, all the deacons of the Trades were members of the Head Court and were equally unlikely to embrace the idea of any radical change that might upset harmony among themselves.

Despite the local endorsement of the status quo, the majority of the Trades decided to go to even higher authority to ensure that there would be no risk of a recurrence of such a case. At great expense their convener, Nicoll and another craftsman, James Whyt, later also to be convener, were sent to

9

Edinburgh to procure ratification of the act of the Head Court by the Scottish parliament. Their costs of £297.6s.2d. Scots included £42.6s.2d. for water freight and horse hire, £120 to the Lord Register, £31.6s.6d. to the King's advocate and £29 to his solicitor plus fees (bribes?) to their servants.[1] As they obtained the requisite act of parliament[2] including in its clauses one authorising the fine threatened earlier at the Head Court on any who tried to make any similar alterations in the future, presumably they considered the expenditure was justified. The town authorities had remarked that the order of precedence among the Trades had been held 'past memory of man' but do not attempt to explain how it was decided.

It is perhaps worth noting here that most of the sums of money in this volume are in pre-decimal terms, pounds, shillings and pence. Twelve pennies made a shilling and twenty shillings a pound. Until the middle of the eighteenth century the Trades used Scots money values. In early modern times, the Scottish pound gradually lost value compared to the pound sterling. By the eighteenth century it was worth only one twelfth. The Scots also used the merk or mark, worth 13s.4d.

Like its predecessor in the Abertay Historical Society publications, *The United Trades of Dundee*, this is a history of the institutions of the Nine Trades and of the individual Trades making up the nine, not of the trades they practised nor the goods they produced, which is another story altogether.[3] From the nature of such a history, it must be told mainly from the records of these institutions and as a result there can be only as much consistency in the treatment of the individual Trades as there has been in their treatment of their records. The treatment of old records and interest in them varies greatly from Trade to Trade.

The Trades' Records

General Monck and other English invaders may have stolen or destroyed much of Dundee's precious archive but they cannot be blamed for the losses of the last 150 years. These are quite as comparable and as damaging and can be attributed to no-one but Dundonians.

When A.J. Warden was preparing his classic book, *The Burgh Laws of Dundee* (1872) it is quite clear he had access to far more information than some individual Trades have been able to produce today. For instance, he quotes an agreement made among the Trades to collect for the poor and decaying brethren. He had found this document in the Cordiners' archive.[4] Today, the Cordiners' clerk has in his care only the Trade's Lockit Books and sederunt book.

On the other hand, a search through the records of the Nine Trades produced earlier records than Warden thought were available. One invaluable find was a MSS written in hands of varying eras bound in blue paper, giving lists and copies of older documents.[5] Another advantage we have over Warden was that the Conveners' Book of minutes from 1698 was discovered in this century providing some of the history before 1756 that he thought had gone for ever.[6] One unfortunate result of the loss of so much archival material is that sometimes Warden is one's only source. Though his energy in transcribing so much of Dundee's archival material rouses nothing but admiration, it is unfortunate that his accuracy cannot always be depended on.

What has happened to the missing papers is sometimes a total mystery. There can be little doubt about one avenue of loss. Various examples both in the Nine Trades and others show that documents held by those acting as clerk, boxmaster, or deacon were not always returned to their rightful owners, the incorporations, on the retirement or demise of these officials. One such occasion arose in 1836 when Mr Patrick Smart, the clerk of the Nine Trades died. His representatives had to take legal steps to get access to his papers. Only when they achieved this, would the Trades be able to get their papers back.[7] And who was to say what might have gone missing in the interval? Even today when the value of such archival material is perhaps more appreciated than sometimes in the past, there can be mistakes in filing and discarding. How, one wonders, did drafts of Nine Trades records find their way into a dustbin in the Hilltown, to be picked up by Anna Macdonald, the local poetess?

Sadly, it is too well known how one incorporation lost its records. Each Trade owns a book kept closely fastened by lock and key, its Lockit Book, in which are entered its secrets such as the rules regulating the behaviour of members and the names of all masters. The first entry in the Fleshers' current Lockit Book, dated 12 April 1870, tells how Mr James Hood Wilson's shop in Union Street was broken into on the evening of 22 November 1869. The thieves had carried away a portable desk containing the Fleshers' Lockit Book, the Boxmaster's intromission books and other papers belonging to the incorporation. The police had been called in and detectives were employed. Advertisements in the newspapers and printed handbills offering a £5 reward were all to no avail. Neither the desk nor its contents were ever recovered.[8] Mr Wilson was the boxmaster at the time but the clerk had had custody of other records so that at least books of minutes dating from 1714 remained in the possession of the incorporation.

The Cordiners were more fortunate as far as their Lockit Book was concerned. In 1940 Mr R.B. Mann found their old Lockit Book in a chest belonging to his father, a former deacon. He very properly returned it to the Trade, thus enhancing their archive.[9] Many similar discoveries must have simply been treated as rubbish by the ignorant or deliberately retained by the finder. It is ironic that these craftsmen particularly should have lost so much of their own history, because their predecessors demonstrated awareness of the problem in 1591.[10] In that year the Trade commented on the 'disorder' that was caused by the loss of their records and decided that an inventory should be made of all of these.

All the material goods that belonged to the Craft, such as mortcloths, the heavy cloth used to cover coffins, and flags, were also to be included in the inventory, which was then to be copied into the Lockit Book. When deacons left office they were to hand over everything contained in the inventory to their successor or replace anything missing. Unfortunately, the 'disorder' continued to the extent that their clerk did not obey the order, at least not to the extent of copying any list into the Lockit Book; if he did it has been lost in rebinding. Thus such good intentions come to nothing.

The clerk of the oldest incorporation, the Bakers, has in his care the old Lockit Books but apart from these only one minute book and an account book dating from the late nineteenth and twentieth centuries documents. Warden was able to quote copies of seventeenth century acts of the Nine Trades he found in the Bakers' possession.[11] The inference must be that some time in the last hundred years, perhaps during a changeover of clerks, there was not a complete handover of documents. It is ironic that in 1913 one rare record, a print of the rules of the Journeymen Bakers' Association dated 1858, was given to the clerk by a previous deacon as he thought the incorporation was a 'suitable custodian'.[12]

The Weavers, in earlier days always reckoned the most intelligent and literate craftsmen, seem to have had a keen historical sense from the beginning. Many of the important documents in their charge in the nineteenth century are still available. The most important of all for each Trade is its Seal of Cause, the letter from the magistrates and council under the town's seal authorising a society to appoint a deacon, and pass rules and regulations which members must obey. It is by virtue of this document that a society becomes an incorporation. The Weavers have never mislaid their Seal of Cause of 1512[13] and their interest is demonstrated by the fact that in 1825 they employed a Mr Home to transcribe one of their old charters. They were so satisfied with the results, for which Mr Home was paid £6.7s.6d.,[14] that the Trade's council felt that as most of their old documents were 'quite unintelligible' – early Scottish handwriting is not easily read –

'there would be a propriety for the satisfaction of the Trade' in having them all written out in a modern hand.

A few days later it was decided to commission Mr Home to make an inventory of the Trade's documents and show what they contained. Those of real importance were to be transcribed at length as it would have been too expensive to make full copies of every old manuscript the Trade possessed. In 1872 the manuscript list was printed, and the printed volume and most of the documents can still be consulted. Since 1980 they have been in the custody of Dundee's City Archivist.[15] The Tailors too have a very full archive deposited on loan in the Dundee District Archive and Record centre.[16]

The story of the Bonnetmakers' records is in a class by itself and can be found in the chapter on that Craft. Suffice it to say here that twice they have rediscovered their Seal of Cause and other important documents carefully packed away and forgotten among their own records. An early Lockit Book of the Glover Trade was found somewhere and donated to Dundee District Libraries by Mr Bryan Lindsay to be carefully conserved by the library c.1990. Where can it have been during the last century and a bit? Warden did not see it.[17]

Even when records are not thrown away or destroyed, there can be accidents. In December 1833, the General Fund Court of the Nine Trades realised that the chest in which older documents were stored had not been opened for many years. As a result the keys had 'fallen aside', a nice euphemism for being lost. Arrangements were made for the chest to be opened and keys for new locks were to be given to the Convener, the Boxmaster, the clerk and two deacons. There is no comment on the state of the contents of the chest, however, once it had been opened.[18]

In all cases where the Lockit Books have been rebound, the binders' and also the craftsmen's ignorance of earlier Scottish handwriting has led to chronological disorder in the pagination. This is unfortunate but not disastrous, unless some of the contents have been sliced off to make a tidy appearance for the binder, as has happened in the first of the Cordiners' Lockit Books.

The late reappearance of the Glovers' older book must raise the question as to how many more records of the Nine Trades may be lying around neglected in chests and attics of descendants of older craftsmen. However, when an appeal was made in the *Courier* some years ago when this history was at an early stage, there was only one response. A St Andrews lady, Dr Fulton, showed me the 1791 indentures of an apprentice shoemaker, William Milne, the son of a bonnetmaker, one of her family, and very kindly provided me with a copy.

The Journeymen

It is important to remember that trade incorporations were formed for the interest of the masters and their families. The welfare of the lower echelons of the various trades was not given a great deal of consideration though masters were usually expected to look after their apprentices. It was assumed that most apprentices would serve their time, become journeymen and eventually masters themselves and then benefit from all the privileges accruing to an incorporation. Few would expect to become very wealthy but the satisfaction of being one's own master, perhaps owning a small business in a small burgh, could be considerable. There was also the safety net of the poor fund of one's craft.

What proportion actually achieved their own businesses is impossible to judge from the existing records. Not all apprentices or journeymen even appear in incorporation Lockit Books[19] but there is no doubt that those who did achieve the status of master were determined to maintain their privileges not only against the unfree but against their servants, the journeymen. It is interesting therefore to find evidence in the records of two of the Dundee Trades, the Cordiners and the Dyers, of associations of journeymen apparently assisted and recognised by the parent bodies. Unfortunately, our only source for this information is Warden, as the records he quotes from have disappeared from the two Trades' archive.

He found that journeymen cordiners had a 'Club' in the eighteenth century. The organisation, whatever it was, seems to have existed under the aegis of the Trade, for on 5 November 1755 John Airth promised to pay the Shoemaker Trade £2 Scots 'as usual'. When John Kidd became journeyman to William Maiden he too entered 'by way of Clubb' in 1726.[20] Another indication that it was a recognised part of the Trade can be found in the entry of 30 July 1723.[21] It was decreed that no journeyman should be employed by masters or masters' widows without informing the deacon, no matter whether the employee was 'stranger, club, or other'.

Warden speculates that the club might have been a way of saving for their freedom.[22] This is a very reasonable suggestion; new masters did not always have enough capital to pay their entrance fee and some offered bonds as security for later payment. Warden's suggestion seems very likely but we cannot discount other possibilities. The club could have been a sort of friendly society specially for journeymen as they did not qualify for support from the Trade's official poor fund. The other possibility is that it was simply a register of Dundee trained journeymen, as opposed to 'strangers', men whose origins were elsewhere. Operating by payments made directly into the Trade's funds, the Club could have been any of these. Unfortunately

14

Warden comments only that 'numerous' subscriptions for 'Ane Club' are entered but gives no further clues. Whatever the Club's purpose, its existence deserves notice in craft history.

Among the Dyer Trade's records Warden also found a book of acts and statutes of the 'Dyer Lads'.[23] Warden first mentions the original book as being in the care of the Dyers and states that he will give all the rules and regulations in full. Two pages later at the end of his section on that Trade, he states that 147 names entered from 1711–1740 were copied from an old book into 'the existing one', which apparently ended on 20 June 1825 with a total of 258 journeymen entered. This is confusing as it becomes uncertain whether he actually examined the original book of statutes or whether there was perhaps another in which the names and statutes were listed.

Whatever he saw, this material seems to indicate that the journeymen dyers like the cordiners had formed an association. Further the rules and regulations which he quotes show that the journeymen were as anxious as the masters to protect the privileges they obtained through serving their time as apprentices with the appropriate year 'for meat and fee' thereafter; and some of them would be registered as journeymen in their Trade's books.

The laws, according to Warden laid down on 15 September 1711, indicate that journeymen paid dues to join the 'Lads' and be recognised as true members of the Trade. The first practical rule, after the general agreement that they should keep order among themselves and preserve all that concerned them, states that 'As we have severally paid out accidents to those who were servants before us, we hereby do determine that any person coming as an apprentice to any master of the said Dyer Trade, shall pay within a fortnight after their entry five shilling sterling, to be disposed of as we think proper in the way of head washing, for which they shall be accepted as a due and lawful comrade and brother'.

This was followed by the statement that 'He shall immediately receive the *word* (my italics), with tokens sufficient to answer that he is lawfully brothered to the trade professeth'. The giving of a 'word' reminds us of the 'Horsemen' of later times and of masonic practices. This impression is reinforced by a later law ordaining that a fine of six pence was the penalty to be imposed on anyone who revealed the 'Word, Chap or Whistle' to any person, apprentice or journeyman, before he was entered a brother.

To ensure that new entrants paid these dues, they were to be ostracised by existing members if their fee was not forthcoming by the end of the fortnight. No entered dyer was to be seen standing, sitting, walking or having any other type of dealings with an unentered servant under pain of a sixpenny fine for every such occasion. This would undoubtedly ensure peer pressure on new recruits but the Lads also decided to appoint 'one principal person' chosen yearly by votes to make sure these 'Acts' were obeyed. It would appear that they termed this person their 'deacon'. Among the forty-odd rules and regulations thereafter quoted by Warden the 'deacon' is to be fined five shillings if he loses or damages the book. Under the heading 'Subsequently added' (Warden's) the deacon chosen is to give 2s.6d. to entertain all the brethren or pay 1s. fine. One has to consider the possibility that this officer was the deacon of the incorporation itself but it seems unlikely that journeymen would feel able to impose such sanctions on the head of their Craft.

Some of the rules illustrate how particular trades could be identified by their clothes. Not surprisingly, dyers were forbidden to wear any undyed woollen clothes but the Dyer Lads were also compelled to wear at meetings a long coat, or 'such a coat as had pleats and buttons at the haunches'. Then red and white strings were mandatory for their aprons. A 2d. fine was due for each omission.

Rules about the behaviour of the lads were similar to those made by masters. Fighting or hurting brother members, and cursing and swearing were frowned on, and the offender was liable for fines of 6d. and 2d. respectively. Revealing trade secrets to non-dyers however was a more heinous offence, meriting a 5s. fine. (These will be Scots money.) On an artisan's wage, these could have been a burden. One sensible order made was that if no fine was imposed for any mistake at the first meeting, the member 'shall be forever free from that fault'.

The majority of the regulations in Warden's second paragraph entitled 'The Laws of the Dyer Lads' refer to work practices among dyers, emphasising the care they must exercise in their trade not to damage the cloth they were working on. Allowing blood from fingers or hands on to the cloth – even allowing one's fingers to be cut! – cost 2d. Practices like using dirty sticks to stir the vats, not cleaning sharpened scissors, or using scissors on different colours without cleaning them first, were all frowned on and could cost the workmen money. There were several regulations which were no doubt aimed primarily at keeping the cloth or thread in good condition but also affected safety. Vats were not to be left with cloth in them, and boiling lead, copper or pewter was not to be left alone.

The founding of such an organisation as the Dyer Lads poses many questions. It may have been an attempt to regularise and control previous traditions when new members were accepted into the group. Initiation rites are still common among all sorts of groups such as the armed forces or

American college students, for example, and sometimes get out of hand. Then again, members already entered who had 'paid their accidents' to their predecessors and experienced 'head washing' in whatever form that took, no doubt wanted to make sure that they gained some recompense from their successors.

It is really impossible to decide whether it was the journeymen or the masters who were responsible for forming the association. Warden gives the Lads all the credit, but the presence of their book of rules among the Dyers' official records must give one pause, as does the mention of the deacon, already discussed. The association may have had the blessing of the masters. On the other hand, the Dyer Lads' book may have been deposited with the Trade at some later date in the mistaken belief that it was in safe keeping with the Dyer Trade, as was that of the journeymen Bakers. The rules about how tools and goods should be handled smacks more of masters' interests than of employees' but without other records the question must remain open. No other records of the Dundee Trades so far seen reveal any such practices and it is a cause for great regret that the original book is not available. The only comparable situation was that among the United Trades.[24]

During the late eighteenth century when interest in radical movements was strong in Dundee, one might have expected more evidence of unrest among workmen than has so far been revealed in the Nine Trades' records. Some journeymen of the Tailor Trade – 'a considerable number' – formed a combination[25] in 1795 which was illegal at that time. In January of that year they demanded that their wages should be raised to 9s. sterling per week, saying they would not work unless their demands were complied with. Needless to say the masters refused unanimously and appointed a committee to prosecute the ringleaders and 'such others as can be known'. The journeymen were not cowed, and the Trade had to apply to the JPs of Forfarshire to decide what the wages should be.

In June, however, yet another combination demanded 9s., scorning the JPs' decision that 8s. was a fair wage. The Trade resolved once again to apply to the courts but agreed to let the men know before they did so. Inflation due to the wars with France soon made nonsense of money values and in 1804 we find a demand for 3s. more per week. Once again the masters thought this unreasonable and agreed they would neither employ other masters' servants nor increase the wages of their present employees. A fine of £5 was to be imposed on those who broke this agreement. But the masters were not completely sure they would win their case and agreed in 1805 that if the Quarter Sessions decided in favour of their journeymen the Boxmaster had to appeal to any other competent court. They had to pay £21.3s.6d. two years later for legal costs in their case.[26]

There is an unconscious revelation of the different standards for masters and men in the Tailor Trade's minutes of 1816.[27] The masters decided on the prices of piece work in proportion to the 14s. per week paid to the journeymen. This was to be intimated by each master to his men in the course of the week and was to begin the following week. The charges made to customers were also to be agreed and inserted in the sederunt book. It is unlikely these masters thought of themselves as being in a combination, legal or otherwise. In November of the year they refused the journeymen's petition for 16s. a week, what their wage had been before the last reduction.

The archive of the Tailor Trade also contains an example of the way in which journeymen could find work. A letter which had been sent to the deacon was reported in the minutes of 29 April 1825.[28] It came from three men, A. Graham, James Dawson and one other whose name was illegible who called themselves the managers of the 'Thistle House of Call'. Houses of Call were often inns where workmen travelling the country looking for work could call in for information about jobs. Though not officially qualified to work in Royal Burghs these 'travelling brethren' were allowed to take work on short term arrangements. This is the only example of this custom so far found among the Nine Trades' records.

The letter informed the deacon that the House of Call for journeymen tailors was now instituted and 'the men is to be found there if required a quarter before 9 o'clock next Monday morning'; interestingly it went on to say 'and the Master is to be denied the use of Weomen', with a hasty note inserted, 'that is they must not be imployed'. The journeymen further tried to restrict the employment of boys, saying they must serve their time, 'even if under two or three masters'. No comment on this approach to the masters was recorded in the minutes, nor does there seem to have been any follow-up.

Journeymen were perhaps prepared to put up with their somewhat inferior lot when achieving the rank of master did not seem too impossible. It is notable that journeymen's attempts to obtain larger wages seem to have become more common in the radical climate at the end of the eighteenth century. At the same time changes in industrial methods were leading to larger organisations in which the opportunities for advancement must have begun to seem more remote than they ever did in the days of the small workshop with one master, a couple of journeymen and perhaps only one apprentice.

Women and the Trades

In these days when equal opportunities between the sexes, at least in Britain, is a matter for legislation, it is interesting to examine the position of women in the crafts. Women have never been allowed to become full members of the Dundee Incorporations. Indeed as we have seen above even their employment as servants could rouse objections from male workers. The United Trades of Masons, Slaters and Wrights countenanced widows as proprietors and managers of their late husbands' business but none of their rules admit the active participation of women in the building trades.[29]

The picture that emerges from the records of the Nine Trades is somewhat different. The nature of the goods produced may be partly responsible for this. In the fifteenth century it was accepted that women might practise some of the trades and even train apprentices. Girls must have served their time as indentured apprentices or their appearance as practising craftspeople – weavers and bonnetmakers, for instance – would not have been countenanced. On the other hand, allowing them to take part in the councils of a Trade either before or after it became an incorporation was probably never even considered.

With this qualification, in four of the Dundee Trades, Bakers, Bonnetmakers, Glovers and Weavers, the existence of women as craftswomen is officially recognised. In the first Seal of Cause granted to the Bonnetmakers on 31 July 1496 the rules explicitly included women. Every woman who could not give the priest a day's meat per week had to pay 1d. weekly instead but only the wives of freemen or one who could carry on with her own resources could be admitted masters. This is not in fact very different from the conditions under which men could join but no women's names appear in the Bonnetmakers' lists of masters.

In the Weavers' Seal of Cause,[30] in 1512 and again in the ratification of 1525[31] their statutes, endorsed by the Town Council, included a similar rule that 'Ilk man or woman who occups ye said craft' and did not give his 'meit' – sustenance – to the priest of the Trade's altar to St Severus should be penalised. In 1512 2s. was exacted to be paid to the deacon plus 2lbs of wax to the altar; in 1525 one penny a week was to be collected by the deacon while servants were to pay a halfpenny. A later statute in each document laid down that no woman was 'as for ane master to hold ane work house' unless she was the wife of a freeman and paid her dues to the deacon and craft like all the other freemen. The insistence that a woman weaver keeping her own work house must be a wife shows that women were not truly full members of the Craft.

Widows were in a separate category, especially widows of freemen of a Trade. The Bonnetmakers made the point that though they were not so privileged as the men they were not exempt from the rules insisting on well made bonnets. On 30 June 1710 after forbidding the use of 'birsel' (dye made from wood of the brazil tree) or 'alm' (alum) on bonnets, they added as an afterthought at the foot of the entry that widows were to be 'finabel as weel as the rest'. The Tailor Trade in 1704 allowed widows to keep as many servants as they pleased to serve the Trade 'as fully as any freemaster'. Like the men widows were subject to the acts and statutes of the incorporation and were 'liable for accidents', i.e. they had to pay the same dues.[32]

But women were not expected or allowed to take any part in the councils of the craft such as electing the Bonnetmakers' deacon. This privilege was laid down in both their Seals of Cause as the preserve of the freemen of the craft who were burgesses. And the burgh of Dundee admitted no free women for many centuries.

In the sixteenth and seventeenth centuries the Bakers regularly apprenticed boys to a master baker and his wife, or the longer living of the two. The indentures recorded in the Lockit Book give both the baker's name and that of his wife. For example, in 1650 Alexander Petrie, son of another Alexander, was apprenticed to William Petrie and his spouse Grisel Gourlay.[33] The right of a baker's widow to keep on a business after her husband's death is implicitly recognised but no women were named as masters.

Only in the earlier Glover Trade's Lockit Book do women's names appear in a list of masters. This statement must be qualified like so much in this history by recognising that we have to remember how much is missing; earlier records of other Trades might have provided the same type of evidence. The Glovers in 1613 and 1615 list four women among 23 masters named and in 1618 one of them Margaret Miln paid 40s.8d. for an apprentice's entry.[34] These women do not appear as officials but they are the only women masters found so far in the records of the Nine Trades. Nor did this custom last. After the first years of the seventeenth century women were as conspicuous by their absence as entered masters in the Glovers' Lockit Book as in any other.

As the journeymen tailors in the depressed 1820s demonstrated traditional male prejudice, always more obvious in hard times, by telling the màsters they could not employ women,[35] women must have been working as tailors' servants. In 1738 Patrick Smyth, a barber in Dundee, promised that his wife Mary Whyte, would not make women's clothes again without obtaining her freedom to do so from the Trade.[36] On the other hand in 1704 master tailors were firmly of the opinion that widows should be supported in work as this would not only help the inhabitants of the town but would enable the women to achieve what they described as an 'honest condition of life for subsisting themselves and their children'.[37]

Women often served as officers of the trade, their main duty being that of delivering messages to all the members. This was another way of providing for indigent widows and children of brethren. Notices of the time and place of meetings, or funerals of brother craftsmen, for instance, were all delivered by hand even after an efficient postal service existed. Not surprisingly women appear regularly as recipients of charity; one of the main purposes of the trades was the care of widows and orphans and the oath of most of the Trades includes the vow that the new member will help to take care of those connected with his Trade.

Receiving help as widows or children of members, not in their own right, women tended on the whole to be awarded slightly smaller pensions than the men. For instance in the 1820s and 1830s in one list none of the women were given more than 6s. while the sums to the men varied from 9s. to 12s.[38] This of course reflects the perennial argument for discrimination in work as well, that men may have dependent wives and families. This conveniently forgets that widows sometimes have to care for children, and single women look after elderly parents.

The twentieth century sees the members of the Trades determined to maintain the official exclusion of women. One member of the Baker Craft, Mr A.D. Buchan, enquired in 1951 if ladies (not women!) were eligible for membership. A year later the acting clerk reported that there was nothing to show that they were not but that it seemed the tradition would be a hard one to break.[39] Despite the passing of the Sex Discrimination Act, 1975, private clubs and societies may still remain single sex so the Dundee incorporations are not breaking any law.

One Trade, which perhaps should remain anonymous, discussed the position before this exception to the rules was clarified. The men decided that they did not want any female members and would simply make it difficult for them to join, if legally they were compelled to admit them.[40] The Weavers were more honest. In 1980 the Hammermen Craft were approached by the daughter of a freemaster asking for admission and they wanted the views of the Nine Trades. The Weavers bluntly agreed they could not support the admission of ladies.[41]

If any wives have been giving curtain lectures to members of the incorporations through the centuries on the subject of sexual equality, they do not seem to have had much effect.

The Trades and the Wider World

One need not look for much information on what was happening outside craft circles or even outside Dundee in the earlier records of the trades. Individual Crafts basically recorded only their own affairs. The Lockit Books occasionally give information about the wider world and then only because a Trade itself has been directly affected. For example plague delayed the election of the Bakers' deacon, David Tendall, from the usual date in October 1585 until 15 February following.[42] The convener of the Nine Trades, John Whittet, presented two years accounts in 1716, explaining that he had had to leave town the year before because of the rebellion.[43]

The eighteenth century wars are mentioned only when the Trades were affected by recruiting policies. During the Seven Years War various groups had to provide men. The Trades sometimes rewarded men who enlisted in their name by booking them free as masters. For example, the Cordiners entered Charles Drummond on 20 January 1757 for joining Colonel Lighton's regiment as their respresentative. In 1778 the Weavers had given £86 which gave the Trade sixteen votes in choosing officers to command a company being raised in the town because of the 'present exigency'. But they do not discuss the issues which caused this exigency.[44]

The late eighteenth century saw a decided change in such introspective attitudes, but the Nine Trades throughout its recorded history has acted on behalf of all its constituent members in most public matters so that relations with the town authorities regularly occupied their attention. By the late eighteenth and during the nineteenth centuries the Nine Trades were very busy making their opinions known on matters that affected craft, town and country. Electoral reform at both burgh and national level is discussed and supported from the 1780s. The move to burgh and parliamentary reform in the nineteenth century found the Tailor Trade agreeing to collect money to support burgh reform in 1819[45] and giving unanimous approval to a petition to the House of Lords in 1831 recommending that the peers should pass the Reform Bill.[46] Strong feelings sometimes emerge too about the Regent particularly and about his wife. In 1817 the Tailor Trade resolved that their deacon should not sign the address to the Prince Regent on his late escape from an assassination attempt.[47]

There are clues regarding economic conditions as Trades reacted in various ways to protect their interests. They might restrict the number of apprentices who could be indentured or make the conditions for qualifying as masters more arduous. The Glovers increased the entrance fee for masters in 1646 to £40 and in 1724 made apprentices pay £30 to be entered. At the same time the years of service after an apprenticeship were increased to four. The Tailors on several occasions imposed a seven year moratorium on the entry of any masters except the sons or sons-in-law of their own free-masters or free apprentices. The Bakers restricted the employment of journeymen by their members in March 1697, during King William's 'ill years'.

As the burgh of Dundee grew throughout the centuries tradesmen became wealthier and more confident and sophisticated. Society also became more democratic and the result can be seen particularly in the wider perspective of the Nine Trades from the inception of reform movements. However too much should not be made of this. During the Napoleonic Wars the question of the alterations to Dundee harbour was discussed but the few references to the war tended to be financial, like the Tailors' £5.5s. for the army of reserve in 1802. The totally different type of the two World Wars fought in the twentieth century meant that they could not be ignored but this is a modern development and outside the mainstream of this volume. Earlier craftsmen had more circumscribed lives and their records honestly reflect this fact.

The End of Craft Privileges

The history of the Trades is still being created but their real influence on the economic and social life of the town ended in 1846. In that year an act of Parliament abolished the trading rights of the Royal Burghs of Scotland and the monopolistic privileges of all trade incorporations and merchant guilds.[48] Though some of the Dundee Trades were still actively pursuing any who tried to practise their craft in the burgh without being members, the majority by that time were not unduly interested in their long-held liberties and privileges. The records of the individual Trades pay little attention to the passage of the act and even more revealing are their re-actions to an earlier bill to do away with the incorporations which had been before parliament in 1837.

A committee of the Nine Trades was appointed to watch over the passage of that bill through parliament. The committee's members consisted of the General Fund Court and three craftsmen appointed by the General Meeting of 4 January 1837.[49] The Edinburgh Trades wanted to press the government for compensation for loss of highly paid privileges, which was not an unnatural request as obtaining membership of a Trade could cost a great deal. But the Dundee incorporations were less than enthusiastic about fighting their corner. The Shoemakers, Dyers and Hammermen disliked some clauses in the bill but were not in favour of taking any steps to defend their exclusive privileges. The Tailors would do nothing at all, the Bakers wanted to oppose the bill and the others, Weavers, Glovers, Fleshers and Bonnetmakers, did not even reply.[50] This seems to endorse the allegation made in the *Report of the Commissioners on Municipal Corporations in Scotland* in 1835 that while there were divided views in many Scottish burghs about the benefits or otherwise of privilege, in Dundee the 'evidence decidedly preponderates against them'.[51] The Commissioners' comment on the flourishing linen trade in the town also may help to explain the Weaver Trade's lack of interest.

The bill of 1837 failed to reach the statute book but nine years later the Trades expressed unanimous agreement with the preamble to the bill that was eventually passed in 1846. It was the end of an old song. Since then the character and aims of the Trades have perforce changed to meet changing circumstances, social and economic. It would not be unfair to say that many of them, though not all, are now more social clubs than charitable or protective institutions. Their story since 1846 has followed a very different track from that of the preceding four centuries. It therefore lies outside any description of their mainstream historic significance. This volume therefore examines mainly the years between the period when the Trades gained recognition as incorporations and the passing of the act that abolished their privileges for all time.

For this apologies are due to those present-day craftsmen who find today more interesting than yesterday but the space available puts restrictions on contents and the period indicated seemed to make practical as well as historic sense. Each of the Trades of the Nine has its own character and particular history but the general aims of all craft incorporations were the same. They hoped to protect their members in work, in sickness and old age, to maintain high standards of craftsmanship and not least, 'to serve the lieges'. These general objectives will be examined in Chapter 2 and the history of the Nine Trades in Chapter 3. Thereafter those aspects of the nine member incorporations peculiar to each will be dealt with in separate chapters, but Chapter 2 is the story of them all.

NOTES

[1] NT4.1, 18.5.1695.

[2] APS ix, 131.

[3] E.g. Enid Gauldie, *The Bonnets of Bonnie Dundee* (Dundee, 1993). Hereafter Gauldie, 1993.

[4] A.J. Warden, *Burgh Laws of Dundee* (London, 1872), 249. Hereafter Warden, 1872.

[5] NT5.2.1.

[6] NT4.1.

[7] NT2.6, 2.11.1836.

[8] FLB – in custody of the clerk.

[9] CSB, 12.9.1940.

[10] CLB1 – in custody of the clerk.

[11] Warden, 1872, 260.

[12] BMB, 30.9.1913.

[13] DDARC, GD/TD/W7.9.

[14] DDARC, GD/TD/W3.1, June 1825.

[15] DDL, GLB.

[16] DDARC, GD/TD/T.

[17] DDL, GLB.

[18] NT2.6, December 1833.

[19] Annette M. Smith, *The United Trades of Dundee*, Abertay Historical Society Publication No. 26 (Dundee, 1987), 17–18. Hereafter Smith, 1987.

[20] Warden, 1872, 389.

[21] CLB1.

[22] Warden, 1872, 389–390.

[23] Warden, 1872, 568–570.

[24] Smith, 1987, 8.

[25] DDARC, GD/TD/T1.1, 102.

[26] DDARC, GD/TD/T1.1, 26.6.1804; 24.10.1805; 17.2.1807.

[27] DDARC, GD/TD/T1.2, 10.4.1816.

[28] DDARC, GD/TD/T1.2, 29.4.1825.

[29] Smith, 1987, 7.

[30] DDARC, GD/TD/W7.9.

[31] NT5.2.1.

[32] DDARC, GD/TD/T6.2, 8, 8.9.1704.

[33] DDARC, GD/TD/B1.1, 212.

[34] DDL, GLB.

[35] See above p. 18.

[36] DDARC, GD/TD/T6.36.

[37] DDARC, GD/TD/T6.28, 8.9.1704.

[38] DDARC, GD/TD/W4.2.

[39] BMB, 29.10.1951.

[40] Reference available!

[41] WMB, 21.10.1980.

[42] DDARC, GD/TD/B1.1, 87.

[43] NT4.1, 11.10.1716.

[44] DDARC, GD/TD/W9.50.

[45] DDARC, GD/TD/T1.22, 7.5.1819.

[46] DDARC, GD/TD/T1.2, 21.9.1831.

[47] DDARC, GD/TD/T1.2, 14.3.1817.

[48] 9 Vict. c. 17 (14 May 1846).

[49] NT2.7, 20.4.1837.

[50] NT2.7, 24.4.1837.

[51] Parl. Papers 1835 [30] xxix, pp. 83–5.

CHAPTER 2

Craft Incorporations

Merchant guilds and craft incorporations were first founded in the growing number of towns that were appearing all over western Europe in the twelfth and thirteenth centuries. The seeds of town growth were often generated in markets so that both the merchants and the craftsmen who prepared the goods to sell soon understood that co-operation would benefit them more than rivalry. Scotland was always part of the European scene though often a 'late developer' and both burghs and their concomitant institutions developed in Scottish burghs. The only difference was that they emerged rather later on the scene. Dundee was one of the wealthiest and most important burghs in the country in medieval times and one that had European connections from a very early date; the early presence of guild and craft societies is to be expected.[1] Though most of the written records of both Merchant Guild and Trades date from only the fifteenth and sixteenth centuries they contain evidence of previous communal activities.[2] Robert I's charter granted to the burgh in 1327 did not create but only revived the Dundee guild so the assumption must be that there was one previously, perhaps temporarily disbanded in the Wars of Independence.[3]

Craftsmen's attempts to discipline themselves and protect their livelihood did not always meet with the approval of the Scottish government. Though an act of 1424 allowed them to appoint deacons, by the end of the century their meetings were thought to 'savour of conspiracies' and in 1493 the 'rycht dangerous' powers of the deacon over the private morals and behaviour of craftsmen in his trade were forbidden by parliament. Not only his powers were proscribed; he was to be replaced by a 'visitor' who was responsible for craftsmanship alone.[4] In the same year almost all craft societies fell into the category of 'oppressors of the lieges' as this was the description given to associations which laid down that no master could finish work left undone by a fellow craftsman. This was an ordinance common to most Trades which helped to prevent undercutting and competition for work among masters.

Six years earlier the crafts had faced a further restriction on their powers when the Three Estates laid down that they could not act as merchants without renouncing their craft.[5] This regulation lasted until the nineteenth century. The Three Estates did at least recognise the important place of the craftsmen in the burghs when the representatives were given a share in electing burgh magistrates and officials in 1469.[6] In 1592 further assistance was given to burgh craftsmen when the Scottish parliament tried to prevent their trades from being practised outside burgh boundaries.[7]

The significance of this last act lies in the close connection between craft incorporations and the Royal Burghs. These were towns that had been presented with royal charters which granted them special privileges, notably in the export trade and in marketing goods within the country. Needless to say there was a price to be paid by the privileged burghs – they had to pay a share of all taxes imposed by the king. This in turn gave them some political power, the expectation that they should have some say in economic matters, however slight, and they became one of the Three Estates of the Scottish parliament. The Convention of Royal Burghs was their own forum which lasted until local government changes in 1975 wiped away the Royal Burghs themselves.

Not all the inhabitants of the Royal Burghs bore part of the burden of the stent, the tax assessment. Those who did were the burgesses, full members of the town community, who not only paid their share of taxes but paid for the privilege. They were the freemen of the towns and expected privileges from the burgh, not available to their non-paying fellow residents, the indwellers, just as the burgh paying royal taxes expected privileges from the monarch. When a group of craftsmen or merchants formed a private society for mutual protection they were also trying to strengthen their burghal position. Such groups sought still greater security by approaching their town council for recognition. This was granted in the form of a Seal of Cause, a letter with the town's seal attached, allowing them to elect a deacon and enact rules that were binding on their members.

It is an interesting aspect of Scottish constitutional history that the power to recognise trade societies as incorporations lay in the hands of the town councils while apparently only the central government could abolish their privileges. The burgh's powers had their limits, however, and the incorporations they authorised had powers only within the burgh. The local incorporations therefore tried to obtain an additional charter from crown or parliament to ensure their corporate identity outside the burgh. Some of the Dundee Trades certainly followed this pattern, the Weavers, the Waulkers, and the Hammermen.[8]

Organisation of the Trade Incorporations

The Seal of Cause allowed the election of a deacon and usually endorsed ordinances already made by the Trade which bound all the corporation's members. These varied and the Dundee examples will be examined in the chapter on each of the Nine Trades. The Trades realised early on in their life as incorporated societies that they needed records of their membership, of their financial affairs and of the rules they made. The records of every Trade were first kept in a special book. The contents of this volume which were indeed 'trade secrets' were kept from any prying eyes by having the book bound very sturdily, usually in wood covered with leather with a metal lock to close it; hence the name of what is usually the most treasured possession of each Trade, its Lockit Book. The key was in the charge of an elected official, sometimes but not always, the clerk or the deacon.

In the Lockit Book were written the rules of the Trade, and the names of masters. The entry of apprentices was also supposed to be included and sometimes the oath all members had to swear. Some of the Lockit Books contained the names of servants or journeymen. However good the intentions of the Trade these records were rarely kept perfectly, except in the case of the entry of masters. The masters *were* the incorporation. Their interests were paramount and apprentices and journeymen or servants had no say in the running of a Trade. Entry in the Lockit Book opened the door of unquestioned privilege within the burgh. No master would have countenanced risking the loss of these by omitting the ceremonial 'booking' of his name as a fully paid-up master.

The ruling official of each Trade was the deacon, elected by the masters. The deacon's powers were potentially great. In 1607 the Glovers imposed a fine of 2s. on any master who ignored the deacon's summons and also forbade swearing in front of him. He could go and examine the work going on in a member's workhouse; indeed in some Trades he was instructed to do so at regular intervals. Masters could be disciplined for not showing him proper respect and he was personally responsible for assessing the need of individuals for poor relief during much of the eighteenth century. This had sometimes to be paid out of his own pocket initially. An elected council assisted him in most incorporations but the main responsibility in between meetings was his.

The boxmaster was second in importance to the deacon but this office did not become common until the seventeenth century. Indeed as late as 1636 the Baker Trade appointed two 'compositors' to assist the deacon in collecting money.[9] As the name indicates the boxmaster looked after a Trade's box in which all fees, fines and artefacts were deposited. Like the

Lockit Book it too was provided with lock and key, often more than one. The keys were then given into the care of several members so that the box could not be opened by one alone.[10]

Each incorporation had its clerk, who had to be literate. The clerk was responsible for making all entries and decisions in the Lockit Book, or later in sederunt books, and for communicating with other bodies and individuals. It is therefore not uncommon for a writer, (a lawyer) often one who was also a public notary, to be employed as clerk. Indeed, in 1557 the Bakers instructed their deacon that he must not allow anything to be inserted in the Lockit Book except by a public notary.[11] By the eighteenth century most Trades in Dundee were employing lawyers as their clerk and today some firms employed during the nineteenth are still serving them. This is not a universal custom, of course, and in some Trades members acted and do act as clerk. Having a lawyer as clerk, keeping records in his office, should make it easier for a Trade to keep track of such documents as their Seal of Cause, than leaving them in private hands, but this has not necessarily been the case.

The clerk usually received some remuneration for his pains and the other paid official was an officer whose duties included that of messenger, taking notices of meetings of the Trades including funerals of members to all masters. Sometimes a new master had to serve for a year as officer but the post was also used as a means of providing for old or indigent masters. Cleaning the Trade's room in the Trades Hall as well as church seats also sometimes fell to his lot. In the nineteenth century widows of masters were often employed in this way but changing circumstances – the loss of privileges, the sale of the Hall, the introduction of cheap postage – lightened their duties to the point of extinction.

The Trades' Finances

The main source of all Trades' funds was initially entry fees, though fines on various pecadillos, major and minor, helped swell their coffers. Though each Seal of Cause contained the condition that a Trade should support an altar in the parish church with a chaplain to say and sing services there, one of the main purpose in collecting as substantial sums as the craftsmen could afford was to provide for their aged, sick and indigent members and for widows and orphans of members. After the Reformation when their altar money was transformed into part-payment of the ministers' stipends, provision for charity for members in need and for 'stranger' poor was perceived as the chief destination of their funds.

All the steps up the ladder within the Trade to becoming master had to be paid for. A new apprentice had to pay a sum to the Trade and give a dinner. In addition the master had to 'book' the new apprentice, that is have his name entered in the Lockit Book, and that had to be paid for. Entry into the Trade as master incurred further expenditure, a further payment to the chosen Trade which included entry fees and various so-called 'accidents'; and another dinner! In hard times when the poor fund was depleted, various Trades exacted extra payment 'and no denner'. The names of newly-engaged servants were also supposed to be entered, again at a price, and the cost of this was sometimes borne by the established master, not by the journeyman.

The 'accidents' were additional payments which varied throughout the history of the incorporations and also between Trades. The Skinners or Glovers, for instance, had to pay towards the house at the East Port kept for treating skins, but some payments were common to all; a contribution to the General Fund after this was founded in 1697; the officer's fee, when the master did not have to serve as such; in earlier days the hospital fee which ensured a master a place in that institution run by the town council in time of need; a fee to share in the Trade's seat in the kirks; all these appeared at times.

The right to the use of a Trade's mortcloth could also be among the dues paid by the master on entry. The mortcloth was a heavy fringed cover, often velvet, which covered a coffin both in the house of the deceased and on the way to the graveyard. All Trades seem to have owned mortcloths of varying sizes and these brought them additional income. A master at his entry had paid only for the right to its use, not for the actual occasion when he or his family might have need of it. They were not cheap. The Fleshers for instance bought a new one which cost £17.7s.0d. in 1770 when their yearly income was between £32 and £40. They paid for it in two instalments but they were charging 1s.6d. for its use in 1773. At that rate their capital would have been recovered fairly rapidly.[12] Keeping this expensive item clean and in good repair was one of the officer's duties and a charge was made on each occasion it was cleaned and hired. As the mortality rate was high in growing industrial towns the poor box benefited greatly from this rather sad possession. Another source of income marked the more cheerful occasion of a master's marriage. Then the marriage merk, 13s.4d., was exacted.

Fines could be imposed for all sorts of offences from bad workmanship to moral turpitude such as adultery or fornication, with minor infringements of statutes of the Trade in between. Most ordinances laid down a series of increasing fines for first, second and third offences. The last often threatened banishment from the Trade but that seems rarely to have been needed, at least to judge from records of the Nine Trades now available.

What should have been an important and regular source of income for the poor box was what were called Quarterly Accounts. In theory each master should have paid in a sum to the boxmaster each quarter. This did not happen. However loyal to their Trade masters might be, they grudged many of these payments, especially the booking of journeymen. This led to complaints at intervals from deacons and also, unfortunately for the historian, to very incomplete lists of apprentices and servants. Throughout the Trades' records there are regular anguished complaints that apprentices are not being booked, that journeymen are engaged without the deacons' knowledge. In 1680 the Bonnetmakers laid down that no master was to fee a servant without informing the deacon.[13]

The Bakers tried in 1699 to regulate and keep better records of such transactions by restricting the time when feeing took place to the week before Palm Sunday.[14] In 1783 the Tailors ruled that no more than eight weeks should elapse between the beginning of an apprenticeship and the booking of the child and they insisted that a journeyman should be booked immediately he began serving a master.[15]

The constant harping on the subject of the failure to make formal note of the entries and employment of these minor members of the Trades with consequent loss of income shows that the problem never disappeared. This is not too surprising. The apprentice's indentures still held good whether his name was in the Lockit Book or not. The journeyman too had little interest in whether his entry was made or not. His master might be fined but he would not lose his job. Probably not all omissions were deliberate. Many masters were literate as can be seen from the many who sign their names from early time, but even so they may well have found it easier to practise the manual side of their business. Boxmasters too whose main business in the incorporation was financial must often have been too preoccupied with their own affairs to chase members who defaulted.

The exactions varied over the years but one principal never changed. Freemen's sons and their daughters' husbands paid less than unfreemen. (No Trade seems to have thought it worthwhile to make arrangements for the wives of freemen's sons.) In the inside cover of one of the Weaver Trade's books the fees due on entry are £8.13s.11d. for the unfree, £4.17s.0d. for sons-in-law and £3.3s.6½d. for freemen's sons.[16]

Alluding to the unfree reminds us of yet another expense faced by would-be masters; however skilled they might be they had to become burgesses, freemen of their burgh, before they could be accepted into deaconry, the phrase used to describe becoming a member of an incorporated trade. One example demonstrating this occurred in 1682 when the deacon of the Weaver Trade, James Hazelles, was ordered not to admit anyone to the Craft as free master until he had agreed with the burgh Thesaurer (treasurer) 'for making himself ane free burgess'. The town's concern about this is shown in the next part of the order. The deacon was to make sure no-one not a free burgess should vote in the election of the magistrates, which was one of the Trades' privileges but not something available to non-burgesses, masters or not.[17]

There was some circular motion in this process. The town council had declared that no-one could be a freemaster in a Trade or a member of the Guild unless a deacon or dean of Guild pronounced him worthy. And no-one could become a freemaster until he was accepted as a burgess![18] From later records it is clear that some slipped through without qualifying as burgesses.

From about the middle of the eighteenth century until the third quarter of the nineteenth it was a common practice for men to join several Trades. They may have started off as straightforward working members of one, but having membership of others seems to have become a fashion. They were not usually categorised as 'dry-handed'. They may have looked on this multi-membership as an insurance in earlier days, as a passport to the poor box in case of need and perhaps as a way of keeping an ear to the ground among all groups in society. Later when Trades divided up their surplus funds, the entry 'fee' was sometimes looked on as a dividend. The Nine Trades recognised the phenomenon by allowing reduced contributions when a master's entry to a second, third or further Trade was notified when the Lockit Books were inspected.

The Aims of Craft Incorporations

Craftsmen of one Trade worked together, obeying rules laid down by the deacon and council they elected, for largely protective and monopolistic reasons. They pursued their objectives by several avenues. As they wanted to ensure steady work for themselves, they first aimed at limiting the number learning a trade by insisting on a long period of training which involved a fair amount of expense. Attempts were constantly made to prevent outsiders, the 'unfree', who it will be remembered had no responsibility towards the burgh, from coming into the town and taking work the Trades considered rightly that of local tradesmen.

Workers who came into the burgh were not in theory allowed to practise a trade within its bounds or even in the suburbs, as we have seen, though it was always a struggle to prevent them. These unfree could offer cheaper services because untaxed and the inhabitants were not always averse to availing themselves of bargains. Members were instructed not to employ unfree nor to 'pack and pele' – deal – with them. Later there were attempts to expel them from the burghs though there is some doubt about the legality of that.[19] Some incorporations inspected places of work to make sure no outsiders were being employed. In the nineteenth century a sort of compromise was reached by licensing unfree craftsmen; this became usual by the 1830s and even then reached only a portion of the incoming workmen in the growing burgh.

One additional difficulty in identifying those whom the Trades called 'encroachers' arose in the eighteenth and nineteenth centuries. Men who had served in the forces were allowed to practise a trade anywhere by an act of Parliament usually passed at the end of any war. Especially after the long wars with France there were a great many demobilised soldiers and sailors around and many craftsmen who were threatened by the incorporations could show they were acting legally because of this.[20]

Elaborate steps were taken to deal with long term entry into a trade. Self-interest was the motive force behind the statutes and ordinances the incorporations passed to reinforce their privileges within the town, but they passed other regulations which were specifically aimed at maintaining their standards and therefore 'served the lieges' well. They always claimed with some justification that such good service was an important part of the work of the incorporations.

A lengthy training began at an early age. A child became an apprentice to a master for a defined period, varying according to the rules then in use in the craft chosen. Indentures included the time he or she must remain an apprentice and then the years that must be served as a servant/journeyman before trying for entry as a master. Time alone did not suffice to obtain this prized situation. The would-be master had to give proof of his competence. The Trade set a test, called variously an essay, say or master stuck, the masterpiece by which he gained admittance. Despite the 1846 legislation the Fleshers failed an applicant in 1876.

Five years apprenticeship with two years 'for meat and fie', that is as a servant, was common but in each Trade we can find exceptions to that rule. Seven years apprenticeship was the specified time in the earliest Glover rules.[21] At times in the seventeenth century the Hammermen demanded much longer periods of training – seven years plus two as servant or eight plus one, and six years was common. There did not seem to be any particular reason for the increased length of time or demands from any specific branch of the Hammermen.[22] In 1730 the Cordiners ruled that four years must be served as a journeyman and criticised the type of essay hitherto offered as 'superficial'. This may have been their response to the town's harsh comments on their work some years before.[23]

As well as insisting on the length of the apprenticeship all the Trades demanded not only careful and thorough training by the masters but care for the apprentice's physical well-being. The Glovers laid down in June 1564 that apprentices could be taken only by a master with a house and a wife plus sufficient meat, drink and significantly 'labour', that is enough work to be able to give a comprehensive training.[24] A few years before, in 1556, the Baker Trade had been even more precise in individual indentures. James Cathrow was to be given 'ane twapenny laif' every baking though he had to provide his own clothes.[25] A few months later David Tendall was instructed that he must teach his apprentice 'every point and neither hyd nor reseill (conceal) na poynt thereof'.[26] Many Trades allowed a master to train only one apprentice at a time. There were two reasons for this. One was that it meant that the apprentice could get full attention. The other was less altruistic; fewer potential masters were in the pipeline.

Similar conditions were repeated by all the Trades throughout the centuries. Such rules were the norm in every Trade's statutes, not the exception, and in return the apprentice was expected to obey the master and serve him loyally. In addition indentures also regularly contained the promise to defend the master against any possible slander and tell him if any 'skaith' (harm) was likely to come to him. Many of the indentures also insisted on regular attendance at church. The penalties for infringing some of the rules were draconian. Absenteeism was frowned on and for any day taken without permission two days were added to the period of apprenticeship. Marriage was practically forbidden and allowed only in very special conditions. The apprentice who was found to have committed the deadly sins of adultery or fornication lost all the time served and had to begin his apprenticeship over again.

Arrangements were made for an inferior class of apprentice who was rarely if ever expected to enter the ranks of the masters. These like the young would-be weaver, Joseph Beard, signed on for only three years and were often given the name of 'bastard' apprentices.[27] As this method of being trained was much cheaper than the full apprenticeship it may have been envisaged as a method of helping poorer children. Usually it was agreed that they could turn themselves into 'free' apprentices but it is impossible to say how many actually did. Most of the Trades recognised this form of entry and many were entered in the Lockit Book.

While such arrangements were occasionally made and children educated by the various local charities were also allowed entry on lower rates, it may be noted that the costs involved in becoming a master were such that the poorest in society were excluded. Parents of apprentices included craftsmen, merchants, professional men, sailors and were not always Dundonians but were not beggars or paupers. Further, while it would be rash on account of the paucity and unevenness of the records to make statistical statements about the level of literacy among craftsmen, it can be said that many were sufficiently well-educated to be able to sign their names. However, the inability to do this did not seem to handicap them and many deacons simply penned their initials at the head of a list of masters' signatures.

The insistence on a good lengthy training period certainly included elements of restriction but there can be no doubt of the craftsman's basic pride in his workmanship. Sometimes standards might seem to slip when perhaps a Trade became slightly careless about masters' test-pieces but such slovenliness rarely became a permanent character of any incorporation's behaviour. Serving the lieges well was too ingrained in their traditions to allow slipshod work to be passed for long.

The Crafts and Charity

One of the main functions of a Trade was to collect funds to provide a safety net for those of its number who could not help themselves. Throughout their records there shines concern for the poor and considerable worry when the funds were too low. Trade incorporations were very conscious of the difficulties faced by ageing or sick craftsmen and their families, either when the husband was alive or when he left widows and orphans. There were few opportunities even for skilled craftsmen to save for the rainy day that almost inevitably came. The established church gave to all the deserving poor of the parish; friendly societies and private charity all provided small amounts to some groups of the needy. The master craftsman and his family could look to his Trade.

Initially relief was given at the discretion of the deacon and he was repaid when he cleared his accounts at the end of the year. Relief could take many forms; financial grants, assistance with rents, coal, clothes were all acceptable. By the nineteenth century regular payments were made by the boxmaster in most Trades and the recipients then are mostly widows or the children of craftsmen. Daughters particularly could be found on the pension roll for many years.

The Tailors on one occasion practised a very practical form of charity. When a Mrs Strachan asked for help in 1813, it was decided to buy her a mangle. There was some doubt as to whether the funds should be used for this purpose. Instead members were asked for contributions with which a mangle of 'very superior size and construction' was bought. Mrs Strachan was to have the use of it unless she remarried, when it would be passed on first to her family and then to other deserving cases.[28] As she seems not to have needed any further assistance, the lady seems to have made good use of the equipment for over twenty years but in 1835 the Trade was very upset to hear it had been offered to a lawyer. The sale was forbidden and three years later the mangle was returned to the Trade and sold.[29]

Recipients were at all times many and varied and not only local. It was customary for centuries for local groups all over the country to help 'travelling' craftsmen, those who were moving around looking for work, usually short-term. As late as 1828 the Fleshers included payment to a travelling flesher in their accounts. 'Stranger poor', that is craftsmen who did not ordinarily live in the burgh, were also legitimate objects of compassion, though of course they did not receive so much; there were bound to be fewer of them, for one thing. In 1733–34 the Weavers paid out £7.6s. to strangers, compared to £105.10s. to their own Trade's poor. One unusual entry was the Weavers' 2s. in 1765 to 'a stranger who had his house burned at Glasgow'.[30]

The 1819 troubles[31] caused the Tailors great worries over their poorer brethren and it is much to their credit that they decided they would give relief as usual despite the problems that might arise from the interdict placed on the Trades.[32] On another occasion not long before this the Tailors also had a private collection from their members and accrued 100 merks to send two blind tailors to see a doctor.

Trades also made contributions to private charitable institutions. One guinea each year to Dundee infirmary was usual. The Orphan Institute received one guinea from the Tailors, two from the Weavers. The Tailors stopped their contribution to the infirmary for a time from 1833, as their funds were so low their poor were suffering. They also refused to support the Public Seminaries at the same time as they thought this was 'inconsistent' with the purposes for which they gathered funds. In 1854 the Weavers gave £5 for the widows and families of men killed in the Crimean War. Unfortunately the poor of all the Trades suffered as a result of the application of funds to the rebuilding of the town's churches after 1841.

In the nineteenth century there were interesting developments in the administration of the poor funds. Appeals came in from all over the world as Dundonians emigrated and found themselves in need in Australia, Ceylon, Canada, South Africa.[33] There was closer scrutiny of applicants too. The Tailors decided in 1816 to send four of their council to visit the poor once a month.[34] One claimant on the Weavers' funds, Widow Chalmers, was decided to be 'not an object of their charity'. In May 1836 'certain information' had been passed to the Trade that she had a large sum between £25 and £35 in the Bank of Dundee. A month later it was reported that she had in fact £20 deposited with the Elders of the School Wynd Meeting House and £9 in her own chest.[35] One wonders just how the Weavers discovered this.

The founding of the General Fund in 1697 gave extra help to the poor of all the nine Trades but there was controversy in the nineteenth century over the lists of their poor which each Trade presented to the General Fund Court. This ended in closer scrutiny by the central body and some indignation among those who were accused of such impropriety. However, the General Fund committee pursued the offenders and the Cordiners and Hammermen were asked for repayment.[36] Despite the development of the Welfare State of the twentieth century, the Trades were still finding worthy recipients for their charity. Modern accounts show that the Bonnetmakers, for instance, were awarding pensions as late as 1980. As we shall see, however, once the privileges of the Trades had been lost in 1846, many came to regard their entry fee as a sort of investment, and care for the poorer brethren received less attention and money.

Products of the Trades

The idea behind having a locked book was to keep the trade's secrets hidden from prying eyes. One 'secret' which seems never to have been entrusted to the Lockit Book was how the craftsmen produced their goods. When the essays for would-be masters, are mentioned, in no trade are they so described that we are given an inkling of what they look like or how they should be made. Sizes and weights and occasionally methods may be specified but that is all.

Glovers had to make double and single gloves to show their skill, but apart from the insistence on properly treated skins being used, the craftsman seems to have been free to design his own. Bakers were subject to town council regulations deciding the size and cost of their loaves. Various types of bread are mentioned, such as semill and wastill, but there are varying suggestions as to what these might be. The *Concise Scots Dictionary* describes Wastill as bread made of the finest flour, or a large scone of oatmeal and wholemeal flour. Warden on the other hand declared that semill was bread of the finest flour and wastill of second quality. But there are no definitions or recipes to be found in the Baker Trade's Lockit Books.

Bonnetmakers from 1525 were allowed to dye the woollen yarn they used and were strictly forbidden on more than one occasion to use inferior dyestuff such as 'bersill' the dye made from the brazil tree's wood, instead of indigo. Like Ford cars, which their maker decreed could be any colour as long as they were black, so Dundee bonnets could be any colour – as long as they were blue. But it had to be a good strong blue. The rival Hilltown bonnetmakers were suspected of using inferior dyes and the Dundee Trade took them before their own Barony court in 1581 to try to stop this. Treating bonnets with alum was also frowned on, but the Trade was plagued with workmen and women who used both brazil and alum. In 1710 the fine was 20s. Scots for first offenders, increasing to 40s. Scots and £3 for any later transgressions.[37]

Nor have any written patterns for bonnets been found in the Dundee craft's records. The processes are mentioned; they had to be 'dichted' (cleaned and dressed) and 'wifed', (woven). 'Weaving' included knitting until quite a late date and was never overtaken by the modern word in the Bonnetmakers' practical records. Finished bonnets were then taken to the waulkmill for fulling. Agreements made with journeymen and servants specify their exact workload, the number and sizes of bonnets and whether they should be dressing or weaving them, but not the method or what the finished article should look like.[38] A selection of these agreements can be read in Warden.[39]

Unfortunately such silence pervades all the Trades' records.

NOTES

[1] E.P.D. Torrie, *Medieval Dundee*, Abertay Historical Society Publication No. 30 (Dundee, 1990), chapter IV; C. Whatley, D. Swinfen, A. Smith, *The Life and Times of Dundee* (Edinburgh, 1993), 10. Hereafter Whatley, 1993.

[2] See comments on Seals of Cause in chapters on individual Trades.

[3] R. Nicholson, *Scotland, the Later Middle Ages* (Edinburgh, 1974), 107.

[4] APS. ii. 234.

[5] APS. ii. 178.

[6] APS. ii. 95.

[7] APS. iii. 579.

[8] NT5.2.1.

[9] DDARC, GD/TD/B1.1, p. 199.

[10] DDARC, GD/TD/W2.1, 9.10.1759.

[11] DDARC, GD/TD/B1.1, p. 7.

[12] FT Account Book.

[13] BtM. Bundle 8.

[14] DDARC, GD/TD/B1.1, p. 48.

[15] DDARC, GD/TD/T1.1, 6.10.1783.

[16] DDARC, GD/TD/W2.2.

[17] DDARC, GD/TD/W1.2, 5.9.1682.

[18] DDARC, GD/TD/T5.4.

[19] NT5.2.

[20] 56 Geo. III c. 67.

[21] DDL, GLB.

[22] HMLB.

[23] CLB. See Chapter 3, The Trades and the Town.

[24] DDL, GLB.

[25] DDARC, GD/TD/B1.1, p. 4.

[26] Ibid., p. 5.

[27] DDARC, GD/TD/W2.1, 23.1.1760.

[28] DDARC, GD/TD/T1.1, 4.8.1813.

[29] DDARC, GD/TD/T1.3, 15.5.1835; T1/4, 28.5.1838.

[30] DDARC, GD/TD/W3.1, 1765.

[31] See pp. 45–47 below.

[32] DDARC, GD/TD/T1.2, 11.6.1819.

[33] DDARC, GD/TD/W.20, 6–17.

[34] DDARC, GD/TD/T1.2, 22.7.1816.

[35] DDARC, GD/TD/W2.2, 3.5.1836, 2.6.1826.

[36] See pp. 51–55 below; NT2.7, 7.12.1826.

[37] BtM Accounts Book.

[38] Ibid.

[39] Warden, 1872, 455–458.

CHAPTER 3

The Nine Trades – 'Nine in One'

Though the 'Nine Trades' as an institution has been officially recognised in Dundee for at least three centuries, there is no document in existence such as the individual Trades' Seals of Cause giving it specific powers to act as a corporate body. The mutual interests of the Trades however must have led them to acting together voluntarily at an early date. The first recorded instance of the fruits of such co-operation is a Decreet Arbitral of 27 September 1527 settling a disagreement between the Guildry and the Trades.[1] The Guildry had obtained recognition of their privileges in what is generally known as the 'Merchants' letter' in 1515,[2] giving powers to the Guildry which the craftsmen thought infringed the privileges they had already obtained.

All the Trades which now comprise the Nine were named in the Decreet except the Dyers who became part of the society only after their union with the Waulkers in 1693.[3] It is also interesting to find that the three Trades still standing first in order of precedence among the Nine had to pay more for setting up booths to sell their goods than other crafts. Skinners, Bakers and Cordiners, mentioned in that order, were to pay 40s. plus 'certain' wax for the church as opposed to 2 merks (26s.8d.) and one pound of wax due from others. The Decreet also left room for expansion of the number of Trades, talking of the 'remanent of ye craftsmen sick (such) as . . .' and then mentioned the other six who eventually comprised the Nine.

The Trades may well have met in the following years to discuss matters of mutual interest but it is almost half a century later before the records of anything of the kind are to be found. In 1568 the provost and town council attended the election of the collector,[4] in accordance with a decree of the Head Court of October 1556 that all such important elections should be carried out in a public place in their presence. In February 1573 the Glovers seem to have convened a meeting apparently designed to restrict the number of apprentices a master could take.[5]

All the Nine Trades attended this meeting and the deacons signed or made their mark to show their agreement, as did the collector, showing that by then the Trades were electing a sort of chairman. Two years later in June 1575 seven deacons passed an act which was to be registered in the common court book of Dundee, with the Commissary Court of St Andrews and in the books of the Lords of Council and Session.[6] It aimed among other things at gaining 'amity and concord' among themselves.

The deacons decided on several rules for managing the Trades on this occasion. A collector was to be elected to settle all debates and strife among the Trades. He was to be a man of good name who was not to communicate or vote – the act does not say where but presumably the town council is meant – or discuss any matter concerning the Trades without their consent. Neither was he to agree to any innovations which might affect the Trades' privileges. This applied also to deacons. Fines to help the poor were to be imposed on any who contravened the act. All disputes between Trades were to be taken to the collector and all were to defend each other, particularly regarding the dispute that was going on between town and Baker Trade at the time. The Glovers and Hammermen did not sign this act.

How the collector had been appointed previously is uncertain but this decision of seven of the nine leaves no doubt that thereafter the official was to be the Trades' choice. Being collector, later deacon-convener, laid heavy burdens, both administrative and financial, on the men appointed. On 14 June 1693 the Scottish parliament had passed an act forbidding town councillors or magistrates to incur debts unless merchants and deacons of crafts agreed. One of the results of this was that after two meetings of Dundee town council on 31 May and 2 June 1698 it was agreed that the convener should be an auditor of all the town's accounts relating to the public or common good in all time coming, the Guildry's accounts alone excepted.[7] This must have made heavy demands on the convener's time. It also gave cause for controversy between council and Trades in the future.

Conveners also had to possess what seemed like bottomless purses. They bore the cost of the Michaelmas dinner when elections took place until 1696. The cost that year was £133.19s.6d. Scots. The annual accounts were usually cleared *after* the dinner, which makes one wonder how carefully they would be scrutinised. Conveners also had to lay out money on casual expenses such as day-to-day poor relief over the year or clothing and shoes for the Trades' officer, and it would seem even major sums such as those needed for repairs to the Trades' Hall.[8] Certainly the money was repaid but in October of 1809 the clerk to the Nine Trades was instructed that in future he was to pay the convener's bills when they were presented to him. It was remarked that it was a 'hardship' to have to wait a year.

Despite this there was apparently little difficulty in finding candidates. When on 14 December 1699 the Trades decided to limit the time that one man should be deacon-convener to two years, they felt they had to add a clause fining anyone £40 Scots who stood for election in a third year; Trades who supported him had to pay £10. The 'factions and animosities' raised by annual elections were deplored but equally, restricting the period of office was expected to alleviate the burdens on those who had been in office for many years, 'which doeth very much prejudge (prejudice) them in their own private affairs and business'.[9]

Many of the earlier statutes and agreements were not signed by all the deacons but it is possible that no significance should be attached to the occasional absence of a Trade's signature from such agreements for there is no consistency in attendance or lack of it. In 1572 the 'haill deacons of craft' accompanied the collector when he claimed through old custom one fifth of timber left on the shore by a Norwegian ship.[10] Almost ten years later in January 1582 the Bakers did not sign the act ordering collector and deacons to agree to nothing which might damage the rights of craftsmen. This incidently decreed that in future a majority vote was to decide matters, the minority having to submit.

In 1683 the title of convener displaced that of collector,[11] and it was laid down that deacons elected to the town council must report to the 'Convener Court' if anything was done in the council relevant to the Trades' interest. Warden quoted the Guildry records of 1685 as mentioning the deacon-convener though an entry of the Nine Trades of 18 May 1695 gives only the title convener.[12] However the full title is certainly in use by the end of the seventeenth century.

The Trades both singly and as a body, even if not yet known as the Nine, played an important part in the life of the community, socially, economically and politically. All the deacons seem to have attended the Head Court from its inception, and two town councillors were elected from the Trades until 1603 – three thereafter. Their position was not always enviable but the whole relationship between Trades and council over the years will be examined later.

Within each Trade we have seen that care for the poor, the sick, the widows and orphans among them was one of their main, perhaps their primary concern. The fact that the first elected official of the Trades was given the title of collector seems to indicate that money is involved though it was not mentioned in the earliest documents quoted. Later, though there is no word in these earlier records of a poor fund or of a box, some of the fines imposed were stated as being designed to help the poor. In 1603 according to a document belonging to the Shoemakers, seen by A.J. Warden but now apparently missing,[13] the collector and all nine deacons decided that they needed a 'subsidy and contribution' at that time beyond what new entrants to each Trade already paid. This seems to show that there were funds collected from the Trades.

The point was made that the Trades bore a great burden 'not only in the common affairs of the said burgh and for the advancement of the commonweal thereof' as well as providing poor relief to their brethren craftsmen. This new fund does not seem to have been aimed merely at poor relief but at helping the Trades bear their general expenses. The usual sources were to be tapped whereby the Trades obtained income, such as payment by apprentices and new masters when they entered the Trade or when they married, and fines for offences such as adultery. The Bakers had imposed a moratorium on taking any new apprentices, a usual sign of hard times, but they had to make contributions as if they were still enrolling boys.

No administrative machinery was provided whereby the collector could enforce the conditions of this statute. Good will and general agreement among the Trades must have been assumed sufficient but it was to have the full force of a decree of the magistrates by being entered into the burgh books. And for almost a century it did indeed seem to be reasonably sufficient but King William's 'ill years' in the 1690s were to bring about a significant change. Those years saw crops failing with depressing regularity, not only in Scotland. The resulting poverty, starvation and disease which affected the great majority of Scots, laid far greater demands on the funds used to provide poor relief, both national and local.

The Dundee Trades tackled their difficulties in times of economic troubles in different ways. Each craft had its own methods of dealing even with the major crisis of the 1690s. The Baxters for instance tried to protect their own members' work by decreeing in 1697 that no journeyman could come into the burgh to work, as freemasters and their apprentices were well able to cope with all the needs of the burgesses. The only help allowed was the labour of young boys to fetch and carry – meal and water to the bakehouse, and the baked bread out to customers. And no unfree lads were to be allowed to take part in any of the baking. Offending masters who allowed this were to be fined £20 and the servant £5. This ensured that the number of bakers in the burgh remained steady.[14]

The magnitude of the crisis, however, forced the nine into making special provision for their poor. The accounts for the 1690s include far more payments by the convener than was usual.[15] At a meeting of all the Trades in the Howff on 29 December 1697 they decided to set up a joint fund, specially to provide extra help for the poor of all the Trades. Every new master had to pay 12d. for every £1 he paid his Trade, as did every apprentice when he was booked, except free master's sons joining their father's Trade. A merk of 13s.4d. was also due on marriages and fines were expected to swell what became known as the General Fund. A boxmaster was to be appointed from among former deacons.

The original plan was that the money should be kept in a box until it reached the sum of 300 merks (£200). Then the convener and deacons were to invest it – 'lay it out upon rent' – and distribute the interest among the poor of the Trades. By the time the accounts of the boxmaster, William Duncan, were audited on 4 November 1699 it was realised this was unrealistic in light of the continued dearth, and the regulation was abolished. The convener and deacons were given absolute discretion in managing the fund for the benefit of the poor. Each individual was to be treated according to his needs, not according to the proportion which a Trade's numbers might seem to deserve. Practical help was given to the officials by authorising payment of 40s. to the convener's officer to assist them in collecting the contributions from the various incorporations.

The agreement made at this time is usually described as the constitution of the Nine Trades but it could be argued that the arrangements made in 1603 deserve consideration as the first, or at least the first known formal union of the nine incorporations which regard themselves as 'Nine in One'. At the earlier date the money collected was for general purposes of the incorporations. In 1697 the only purpose authorised was the support of the poor and there was to be in the future some agonising among members when the general fund was used for anything else.

More sophisticated administrative arrangements were certainly made in 1697 but almost a century had passed since their earlier ordinance. During that century tradesmen had experienced civil wars and revolution, and may have become more aware of the need for more detail in such arrangements. There is plenty of evidence to demonstrate that the Trades had been acting together before this date, and the election of a collector or convener with some authority seems to indicate that a society was formed long before 1697. The formation of the general fund in that year was a response to the exigencies of the 1690s.

One of the effects of establishing this fund was that the Nine Trades as a society became property owners which does not seem to have been the case before. Before banks were every-day institutions buying and renting property was one of the simplest ways of preserving capital and obtaining an income from it; until fairly recently as a result interest was termed rents.

There is little point in giving a long detailed history of the Nine's transactions in town and country property but it is worth noting that possession of the building in Victoria Street came about through the establishment of the general fund for relief of the poor of the Trades in 1697. The premises became the Trades' property outright in 1893 and after various tenants, alterations and improvement are now the headquarters of the Nine Trades.[16]

The management of the general fund became more formal as the years went on. In 1727 the Trades decreed that anyone in debt to them was ineligible for the post of deacon or boxmaster to his Trade without security, which meant in effect that no debtor would be dealing with the general fund, a sensible precaution.[17] The name 'Convener's Court' had appeared by 1742. In 1763 it was decided that the fund should be managed by the present convener, all his predecessors, the nine deacons and their immediate predecessors. Apparently this was arranged without obtaining the concurrence of a general meeting of the Nine Trades, which made it of dubious legality.[18] The alternative title to Convener's Court became the Eighteen Court[19] and the convener's accounts seem to have been audited by this body.

In the political climate of the next sixty years the slight vagueness of the management and apparently the irregularities that crept in provided an excuse, perhaps to the more radical among the craftsmen, to tidy up their administration. In 1819 a revision of the bye-laws was proposed. The committee appointed for this purpose took its duties very seriously and investigated all the records it could find, and discovered that the Convener Court was assuming more authority than it should have. There had actually been a court case against convener Alexander Watt; in 1790 he had appointed a clerk to the Nine Trades in connivance with the Convener's Court against a majority vote of the Trades.[20] Property was being bought and sold without reference to general meetings; unwarranted innovations had been made such as changes in the numbers attending the court; it was felt that the presence of all former conveners since 1763 gave undue influence to some Trades; all transactions from about 1775 were 'buried in darkness'. The one redeeming feature was that there were no financial improprieties to report.

The new bye-laws contained the rule that every paid-up member of individual Trades was a member of the Nine and *if* a burgess could vote on all questions. It is not known when it became possible for a craftsman to be a member of a Trade without being a burgess. In addition a sum was due to the general fund, £2 for a freemaster in 1819. Members had to be seated at meetings with their heads uncovered and were not allowed to interrupt proceedings or use improper language. The new committee of management was to be called the General Fund Court with 20 members, who would include the present Convener and his immediate predecessor, the nine deacons and another representative from each Trade. The moneys available were to be 'judiciously divided' among the poor, which mirrored the clause in 1697 which implied that the needs of individual paupers should be considered, not the size of each Trade. Regulations regarding the time officials could stay in office, the dates of meetings and other necessary administrative matters were also dealt with.

Much of this would seem unexceptional, but the passing of the bye-laws in April 1819 by six to three Trades and by a large majority at a General Meeting in August of that year provoked the most bitter internecine battle the Nine Trades have ever experienced. One of the strengths of the union of the nine was that the interests of the individual Trades did not overtly conflict. Fleshers and skinners might have differing views about treatment of skins of slaughtered animals; tailors, weavers and dyers could disagree over the finishing of materials; the Bonnetmaker Trade took the Skinners to court in 1611 over the measure they used for wool[21] and objected to the Tailors' making cloth bonnets. In the main, however, there was little need for confrontation. Now the Trades with fewer numbers saw their position among the Nine threatened.

Fleshers, Glovers and Waulkers/Dyers took out an interdict to stop the business of the Nine being carried out under the new rules.[22] This course of action meant among other things that no poor relief could be granted and the nine perforce had to revert to working under their former rules. One of the complaints of the smaller Trades was against the custom that had grown up of taking decisions in common hall, with members voting individually. They wanted to return to the older habit of having a single vote from each incorporation. Outnumbered by the other six who had 336 members in August 1819 compared to their 19, four glovers, twelve fleshers and three dyers, their sentiments are understandable, though perhaps not logical in a democratic society.[23]

The protestors also strongly criticised the methods of allocating poor relief. During the various proceedings they tried to argue that the poor of the larger Trades received more than was their due but they found themselves with a poor case there. An abstract of the amounts paid into the funds from 1697 included the tax on meal bought which automatically meant that the larger Trades contributed more. That did not explain why for 72 years nothing was entered from the Flesher Trade; for 71 the Glovers paid nothing and the Waulkers had paid nothing since 1773.[24] Even though they did not share in the common purchase of meal some ordinary fees must have been due.

James Chalmers in his *Report* insinuated that what had really worried them was that they had been claiming for poor relief from the fund far above what they were due.[25] Whatever the rights or wrongs of his statement, there was more careful examination of the lists sent in by the Trades thereafter and on occasion offending Trades had to repay any payment to a person the General Fund Court reckoned was not a proper recipient.[26]

The case was not finally concluded until 1826 when the Court of Session decided in favour of the majority. The committee that had been handling the whole sorry affair resigned and sent a letter read on 9 August 1826 expressing their anxious wish that the Trades would continue to act together and would henceforth not lose sight of their motto 'Nine in One'. The case cost the Trades a great deal of money. It was proposed that the expenses of the case should not be paid from the funds of the individual Trades and it must have been somewhat galling to have the Dyers protest the next week at such a use of the General fund! The poor also were deprived of a great deal of help but those on the list were given 5s. each in August 1826[27] in compensation.

In the course of the next 150 years minor alterations and additions were made to the bye-laws as need arose. In 1831 the proposal by James Chalmers that the convener should be elected by the votes of all members in common hall instead of by the deacons was carried unanimously. The motion that this should be submitted to the Trades to consider separately was lost.[28] The rules were revised once again in 1880.[29] The position of convener elect was introduced in 1975 but it was not until 1977 that the Nine Trades thought that the 1819 constitution established with such difficulty should be reconsidered in its entirety.[30]

The reasons for change were partly financial but took cognisance of the fact that social conditions under which the Trades and the Nine Trades had been founded were different. Also the administrative infra-structure under which the Nine Trades had operated for centuries no longer existed. Dundee was not a burgh and members were not burgesses. Many of the various boards on which the Trades had served had gradually disappeared – the Harbour Commission, for example. The auditor was also concerned that the requisite percentage of their income was not now being spent according to the rules laid down for charitable institutions.

Eighteen months later on 18 April 1979 the new rules were presented to a meeting of the Trades and unanimously approved. The main administrative changes were that the old title of Collector was bestowed on the deacon-convener elect and a Master Court was established, elected by the General Fund Court, to deal with routine matters. Its members are the deacon convener, the collector, the preceding deacon convener, the auditor and four other members of the Trades.[31] It was realised that it was becoming increasingly difficult to realise the original charitable purposes of the Nine Trades. Other charities were in similar position. The 'poor' were no longer so easily identifiable, and though pensions were still being paid in the 1970s the numbers dropped from 95 in 1968 to 11 in 1974.

Education, particularly technical education, was to be one of the main beneficiaries of the changed rules, though the relief of poverty is still the first stated object of the Nine, and this provision gives flexibility to the organisation if times should change once again. In 1980 students were given financial assistance to go to the United States to study catering. The Master Court recommended a grant to the College of Technology for some cases and Dundee High School was awarded prize money. In 1981 scholarships were awarded to students who were refused government or local authority grants because they were embarking on a second qualification which did not qualify for official support.[32]

One interesting and perhaps surprising feature of the Nine Trades' records seen so far is that not all the most treasured traditions of the twentieth century are mentioned. The Bridie Supper for instance, for which the Flesher deacon provides the meat and the Baker deacon the pastry, seems to have appeared by name in the 1950s. In earlier records all the Trades, the Nine and each separate incorporation, talked of dinners – or denners. Nothing was ever said about the menu but the accounts showing the amount spent on drink on all official occasions, from funerals to the convener's meeting with the deacons to decide on how the poor money should be split up, perhaps demonstrate that the liquid intake was more important.

The motto 'Nine-in-One' was engraved on the side of the Trades Hall but when it was first adopted is not officially recorded. Like the particular meeting places of the Trades in the Howff, simply described as their 'usual stanes', some of these traditions would be so familiar to those taking part, that they did not need a written reference.

The Nine Trades has its own flag, often repaired and renewed, showing its coat of arms but the Lyon King at Arms decided that this was incorrect and a new one had to be designed in 1988. There are other ceremonial artefacts. The chain worn by the deacon-convener on official occasions was commissioned in time for the opening of the Trades' Hall in 1778. Badges for ex-conveners were first ordered at the beginning of the twentieth century and in November 1980 a new design was created by the head of the jewellery and silversmith department at Duncan of Jordanstone college, Roger Miller.

After 1846, the Nine Trades had officially no economic influence on the life of the town. Contrary to what might have been expected, however, the innate vitality of the craftsmen and their deep interest in Dundee's welfare ensured that they retained a place for some time in the management of many of its institutions. These have gradually diminished but representatives of the Nine serve on various charitable trusts in the town, notably the Pullar Mortification, the large legacy of James Pullar, who died in 1811.[33]

One notable feature of their activities in the nineteenth century was the widening of the craftsmen's horizons. This is not so well illustrated in the individual Trades' records but must surely reflect the life of them all. They showed their interest in the wider European scene when they presented an address to Garibaldi during his visit to Dundee in 1864, which expressed their 'approval of the noble and patriotic stand he had made in the cause of liberty'. Almost every movement of importance relating to either local or national issues received their attention and they were active in expressing their support or opposition on subjects as diverse as the relations between George IV and his queen, the repeal of the corn laws, a railway between Edinburgh and Glasgow, penny postage, the appointment of an additional sheriff substitute for Dundee, proposed improvements to the town in 1912 to mention only a few. There can be little doubt that the Nine Trades remained a force to be reckoned with long after the demise of craft privilege.

NOTES

[1] Warden, 1872, 97–101.

[2] DDARC, GD/GRW/G1.1, ff. 1–4.

[3] See Chapter on the Dyer/Waulker Trade.

[4] NT2.3, 1568.

[5] DDL, GLB.

[6] DDARC, GD/TD/W7.12.

[7] NT4.1.

[8] Ibid., 1805–06, 9.10.1809.

[9] Ibid., 14.12.1699.

[10] DDARC, GD/TD/W29.11.

[11] NT2.3, 8.10.1683.

[12] NT4.1, 18.5.1695.

[13] Warden, 1872, 249–251.

[14] DDARC, GD/TD/B1.1.

[15] NT4.1, 1690 Accounts.

[16] NT2.1, *passim*.

[17] NT4.1, 11.9.1727.

[18] NT2.5, 17.4.1819.

[19] Ibid., December 1763.

[20] DDARC, GD/TD/W2.1, 29.3.1790.

[21] BmT, Bundle 8.

[22] NT2.5, 29.11.1819.

[23] James Chalmers, *Report, Code of By-Laws, Extracts of Minutes and Remarks on the Constitution of the Nine Incorporated Trades of Dundee* (1839), 24. Hereafter Chalmers, 1839.

[24] NT2.5, 27.4.1819.

[25] Chalmers, 1839, 36.

[26] NT2.71, 4.11.1839.

[27] NT2.6, 9.8.1826.

[28] Ibid., 2.9.1831.

[29] Ibid., Copy stuck inside cover.

[30] NT2.2, 18.10.1977.

[31] Rules and Regulations of the Nine Incorporated Trades of Dundee (as revised 1979). Thanks to Mr D. Richardson for providing me with a copy of these.

[32] NT2.2.

[33] NT5.19. My thanks are due to Mr D. Goodfellow for information here.

The Nine Trades and the Trades

The Nine Trades as an institution holds an ambiguous position *vis-à-vis* its constituent members. Rules cannot simply be made by its ruling committee or even at its general meetings telling each incorporation how to conduct its internal affairs. From the start of their uniting for the benefit of all, the agreement of each Trade expressed through the deacons was necessary before joint action could be taken or orders given regarding the behaviour or management of one or all the nine.

However, the control of the General Fund from 1697 gave the organisation the undoubted influence that arises when financial management is in question. The care of the poor of every Trade was enhanced by the inauguration of the fund and it would have been a foolhardy or very wealthy incorporation which would have risked damaging the prospects of its most vulnerable members. It was of course a two-way process. The deacons on the Eighteen Court still had to have the agreement of their Trades before any radical policies could be carried out. The Convener Court's neglect of this elementary fact dating from the late eighteenth century was one of the reasons for the damaging dispute between the smaller and larger Trades in the nineteenth.

Financial control, though perhaps influence is a word more acceptable to member Trades, was certainly exercised. Trades had to show their accounts and the Convener Court could and did investigate these. It was only in the mid-nineteenth century that the General Fund Court decreed that only Lockit Books need be endorsed each year and this is still the case. Oversight of accounts and Lockit Books was justifiable as subscriptions from the individual Trades for each member were the only original source of income for a fund that was to benefit the poor of them all. Of course the General Fund had soon to buy property as the normal method of obtaining a return for money at the time and this provided income too. However, the managers of the General Fund have never lost touch with their origins and even today, new entrants to Trades automatically pay their contribution to the Nine.

The abolition of privilege in 1846 did not remove this element of control, though it was not always accepted graciously by the separate Trades. In 1849 a committee of the General Fund Court was investigating the funds of the respective Trades to make sure that the money given to each had reached its proper destination, the poor. The Baker Trade was called first, as befitted its rank, but no baker appeared though the investigators waited 'a considerable time'. The Weavers objected to the whole process in a letter which the General Fund committee considered 'disrespectful and flippant'.

The demeanour of Mr Fairweather, the Weaver Trade's deacon, was also criticised with 'decided disapprobation'. As he had first denied having a Poor Book and then produced one, the General Fund Court's irritation is understandable. When the Fleshers refused to appear, doubts were also expressed about the regularity of their proceedings.

All the trades eventually made their returns, however reluctantly, and there seemed little doubt that in fact the poor lists of several were fraudulent. The Weaver Trade was very truculent about the whole affair, arguing that none of the present office-bearers had been involved in admitting the dubious cases. Going further they made the point that the General Fund Court had ultimate responsibility and was therefore at fault. It appeared however that they had been claiming for a Euphemia Smith for eighteen years after the correct claimant had died. The Fleshers and Glovers had also some irregularities in the management of their poor. Undoubtedly the General Fund Court had grounds for its worries about the poor funds.[1]

Some years before, in 1764, the Weavers had been in trouble when it was discovered that they were owed money which did not appear in their accounts. Their excuse was that the £30 missing had been spent on meal, which members were expected to repay, but the money had not been forthcoming.[2]

The meal referred to was oatmeal bought in bulk to obtain a good bargain for craftsmen. The Nine Trades as an institution basically acts for itself but there was one venture which it apparently entered into at an early date after 1697 for the mutual benefit of all the incorporations. This was the practice of buying meal in bulk, meal being the staple part of most diets for many centuries. Many Trades found this useful, members having to pay less for the share of a large consignment often brought into the town by sea, than they would have had to find as individuals.[3] Some of the nine Trades at least had been involved in this practice on their own account. The Tailors had bought oatmeal from the Bakers for 483 merks 6s.8d. in 1642.[4] That amount, just over £322 Scots, bought a lot of meal. It seems likely that the Baker Trade with their professional connections had found it easier to make a large purchase and pass on the benefits to their brethren in other Trades.

Later available references mention the 'Trades' meal'. The General Fund committee or its agents negotiated for all the Trades. In 1714 the Fleshers record paying their share of the Nine Trades' meal but they instructed their deacon in October of that year that he must not buy more than the Trade's proportionate share without consent 'within the shambles', that is agreed by the whole Trade.[5] Apart from the savings engendered the General Fund benefited as the merchant supplying the meal often had to give an extra boll (about 56lb) for the poor and each Trade had to pay so much, sometimes merely 1d. per boll, sometimes more, depending on the needs of the fund. In 1772 the Tailors paid 1s.8d. per boll into the 'poor fund' but that was for their own box.[6]

While there can be no doubt of the advantage that cheaper meal must have been to individual purchasers, the whole process was a great trial to the organisers. A deacon might agree to take a certain amount but then find that members refused to take their share, perhaps because they could not afford the larger capital outlay. He could not then compel them to do so.[7] There were continual problems such as the Weaver Trade experienced. They instructed their boxmaster two years after their trouble with the General Fund committee to collect payment when meal was delivered.[8] The Tailors complained of 'confusion' in collecting payment and empowered the boxmaster to take someone else with him in 1772. As a result they had to pay the lawyer, David Jobson, for his help and that must have done away with some of the savings. That same year there were disagreements about the fairness of the division of the meal among members.[9]

Other problems appeared when for instance 100 bolls were bought but only 94 received. In 1709 Lady Edzell had to be compensated for 2½ bolls 'lost' among the Trades. She was paid £8.6s.8d.[10] In 1717 meal failed to arrive and court action was necessary.[11] The Fleshers decided to give up joining in the bulk purchase in 1756 and this meant more for the other eight.[12] Insuring the meal which could be very valuable added to the cost. A shipload of 600 bolls coming from Portsoy from the Earl of Findlater's estates costing £300 sterling was definitely worth insurance.[13] The variation in Scottish weights in different parts of the country could also lead to problems. The Earl's weights led to a shortage of three bolls in 1765.[14]

Despite all the difficulties, however, the benefits must have been seen to outweigh them, for the custom continued until the nineteenth century, though by then several of the Trades had given up taking a share of the purchase. The General Fund had fewer small problems in collecting the money due from each Trade than each Trade experienced with individual craftsmen. For the larger poor fund there were more advantages than disadvantages.

Another aspect of internal management in which the management committee of the General Fund, under whatever name it operated, felt it could legitimately interfere was in how Trades entered members. Any Trade that tried to admit members at lower than the normal rates, for whatsoever reason, could be censured. In 1719 strong exception was taken to admitting men only for their life 'secluding children and servants'. This cost the entrant less but he then could have a larger return on his capital outlay if he needed poor relief. This type of entry was forbidden in the future with the additional order that the privileges of children had to be paid for in future.[15] The Flesher and Tailor Trades did not sign this ordinance but this does not seem to have been significant.

The General Fund Court also took exception in 1756 to the habit of 'some Trades' of booking 'dry-handed' masters without taking anything for the general fund. Dry-handed members were those who did not practise a craft; they included men of all sort of professions and craftsmen of any trade except the one they happened to be entering. The conditions under which these men entered usually included the injunction that they were neither to practise their trade nor to employ servants to do so. The interests of their Trade was not damaged by such entries but the general fund clearly was. An act of the Nine Trades was passed to the effect that such entrants must pay £5 Scots and the like sum to the Trades. The relevant incorporation was liable to the General Fund Court for the dues. Significantly the entry in the Convener's book went on to say that deacons must tell their incorporations so that they could not plead ignorance.[16]

The Weaver Trade was in trouble once again in 1763, this time for allowing cheap entries.[17] The Cordiners met with objections from their own members when they resolved to admit adult life members at reduced costs. A general meeting disapproved and claimed that such entry had never been practised. The possibility of false applications for poor relief at the yearly division made by the General Fund Court was one of the nightmarish possible effects conjured up.[18] And considering the later investigation in 1849 this was not such an outrageous suggestion. The meeting proposed that unfree should pay £2, freemasters' sons 10s. and sons-in-law £1.10s. Having appealed to the general meeting the Cordiner deacon though not pleased with the decision had to accept it and it was endorsed later in the year.[19]

The establishment of a united organisation to act for them undoubtedly enhanced the position of all the incorporations when they had privileges to defend. After 1846 that aspect of the Nine Trades' functions was perhaps less useful. However it is likely that the petition to the houses of Lords and Commons in 1831 in favour of parliamentary reform carried more weight coming from the Nine Trades as a body than from the nine separately. It was also useful to know there was an arbiter if relations between Trades soured, though often the intense individualism of the Crafts meant that they preferred going to neutral law courts to submitting to the judgement of their peers who might be prejudiced. The management of the Nine Trades itself also had to be seen to be fair to all, and the 1819 row was a sign that fairness was not at that time in evidence in the eyes of some of the members.

James Chalmers in his *Report* on the 1819 crisis made the point that by joining one society, their own Trade, members actually join two[20] though no-one could join the Nine Trades without being a member of one of the individual Trades. The image conjured up by the slogan 'Nine in One' was that of extra strength, compared on one occasion to the difference between breaking several twigs easily one by one, while the same number tied together would remain whole. There is little doubt that in most matters the Trades prefer to risk standing alone and managing their own affairs, but the ties are still in existence if needed.

NOTES

[1] NT2.7, *passim*.

[2] DDARC, GD/TD/W3.1, 29.11.1764.

[3] Smith, 1987, 30.

[4] DDARC, GD/TD/T6.2, Receipt 7.10.1642.

[5] FTAB 1714.

[6] DDARC, GD/TD/T1.1, 12.9.1772.

[7] DDARC, GD/TD/B1.1, p. 177.

[8] DDARC, GD/TD/W2.1, 6.10.1766.

[9] DDARC, GD/TD/T1.1, 26.3.1772; 12.9.1772.

[10] NT4.1, 1709.

[11] NT5.7.

[12] NT2.5, first page.

[13] Ibid., 22.6.1767.

[14] Ibid., 18.7.1865.

[15] NT4.1, 5.1.1719.

[16] Ibid., December 1756.

[17] Ibid., 26.7.1863.

[18] NT2.5, 5.4.1814.

[19] NT4.1, 23.8.1814.

[20] James Chalmers, 1839, 25.

The Trades and the Kirks of Dundee

The earliest surviving records of each of the Nine Trades all illustrate the strong connection each had with the church. Each Seal of Cause promised support for an altar in the parish church of Our Lady. A priest was appointed to sing and say services at these altars and many of the fees and fines paid by individual craftsmen included a quantity of wax for candles for the church as part of what was due. The connection did not end with the Reformation. The town council, strongly in favour of reform, quickly transferred these contributions to support the new faith. As they declared that God had shown that altars upheld 'idolatry', the sums hitherto spent on 'very manifest wicked and ungodly' altars were to be given to maintain 'faithful ministers'.[1] This was ratified by the Head Court in 1560 and the Trades found themselves paying £67.13s.4d. Scots towards the stipend of the town's ministers, rather more than the £26.13s.4d. that their altars had apparently cost them.

Protestant churches were arranged and furnished very differently from those of the Roman Catholic faith and one of the major differences was that pews were installed. Worshippers had their own pews which they owned and maintained and usually preserved jealously for their own use, allowing no stranger to use their 'sittings'. Each Trade had its own seats in one or other of the churches into which the old parish church of Our Lady was divided after the Reformation.

These were carefully looked after. A cleaner was employed by each incorporation and also often a door keeper. The Tailors employed Mrs Stewart Duncan, their officer, with strict instructions in July 1816 that she was to keep the door to the pews locked until five minutes after the church bell had stopped ringing to keep out possible intruders. The Trades also improved and decorated their seats. The Weavers, for instance, installed a window over theirs in the Old Kirk in 1828,[2] and clusters of lights, 'hearses', were often placed over the particular pews. Decorative panels showing a Trade's symbols were also not uncommon.

For some time each new master had to pay for his right to a seat in the Trade's pew and this did not always include his family. In 1681 the Glovers decided that anyone who brought in his wife, children or servants would have to pay quarterly accounts for them.[3] Gradually, however, the ownership of seats was recognised as an asset, part of the Trade's property, and the income from renting seats added to a Trade's poor fund and general income. The Bonnetmakers' 42 seats, for instance, were valued at £200 in 1819 while the Weavers were paid £17.14s.6d. rent in 1830.[4]

The Tailor Trade decided to roup their seats in 1816 and this provoked strong opposition from nine masters who signed a minute expressing their 'hearty contempt of such meanness'. They believed – wrongly – that the church seats had been meant for widows and the poor.[5] This protest was simply scored out by some of those occupying the seats in the Old Church.

By the middle of the nineteenth century concern was sometimes expressed about the lack of use of the Trades' seats in the Trades' Kirk, St Andrews. In 1834 the Nine Trades decided to draw up a rota, asking members to attend for four Sabbaths, then allowing the fifth 'vacant'.[6] By the middle of the nineteenth century many masters must have owed allegiance to churches outside the established Church of Scotland. It was not to be wondered at that they did not always attend services in a church of whose doctrines they disapproved.

The Hammermen were the first to sell their sittings; the Tailors bought their seats in the loft in the Old Church in 1759.[7] The great fire of 1841 was the catalyst which decided some other Trades to sever their physical connection with the parish churches. The fire occurred not long after considerable repairs and alterations to the Old Church in the 1820s had incurred all seat owners in contributions towards the total cost of almost £3,000.[8] As late as 1836 there were calls on the Trades' funds as all heritors had not paid their share.[9]

In 1841 the town council asked all with rights to pews in the East and South churches if they would take a share in rebuilding these.[10] The prospect of still further capital outlay when some of the Trades' funds were already depleted cannot have been welcome. The Weavers by March had renounced all their rights, though they were quite happy to join the procession when the new foundation stone was laid.[11] In 1845 the Fleshers expressed their wish to sell. The Nine Trades as an institution did not own any part of the churches but the suggestion was made at one meeting that the Trades should consider acting in unison over this matter.[12] However, nothing apparently came of this and the individual Trades made their own decisions.

After much discussion the Tailors decided that they would accept responsibility only for a share proportionate to the sittings they had in the two ruined churches.[13] In 1842 they agreed formally to pay their share of the new East Church[14] and the following year to help provide stained glass in proportion to the number of their sittings.[15] Costs rose, of course, and in 1843 they were asked by the Kirkmaster, the town official responsible for the fabric of the church, for 6s. more per sitting than the original £4.14s. estimated to pay for installing heating and fitting gas brackets, among other things.[16]

Once the East Church was in use again the process of letting began again. The Tailors had 52 seats, which they let at various prices from 6s. to 15s. a seat, depending on how much the members of the congregation were prepared to bid.[17] They also contributed to rebuilding the South Church though they became rather worried about the increasing costs of the plans. In December 1873, however, they too began the process of selling their seats to the church itself for £100,[18] but it appears that it was 1880 before a final agreement was reached.

All this time the Trades were contributing to the stipends of the ministers of the parish churches. The General Fund of the Nine Trades also contributed £2.17s.3d. from the middle of the seventeenth century. An appeal from Dr Davidson in 1801 pointing out how little this amounted to in 1801 led to a rise to £10, though it was emphasised that this was solely on account of his merits and would not bind the Nine Trades to paying his successors such an increase.[19]

As important constitutionally in the town, the Trades were represented by the convener and deacons during all important ceremonies in the churches. For instance they joined the town council in 1699 when a new minister, Mr Samuel Johnstone, was admitted to his charge in the parish churches.[20] The close connection between the town kirk and the Trades was weakened, however, by the building of St Andrew's, the Kirk in the Cowgate, in the 1770s. Built by money raised by the kirk session of Dundee and the twelve incorporated Trades, the Nine and the United, this is still known as the Trades' Kirk and in October, each year, after their yearly meeting to elect officials, the Trades attend their 'kirking' there, the yearly service of dedication.

For much of the eighteenth century there were three parish churches in Dundee, all in care of the town council, with a joint kirk session. Though there were episcopalians and seceders in the town with their own places of worship, the session was very aware that the rapidly growing population needed another church attached to the Church of Scotland. In 1770 the Nine Trades agreed to raise one third of the necessary money, with the help of the United Trades who were to provide one quarter of that third. The kirk session was prepared to find another third and it was assumed the town council would be responsible for the remainder.

This last assumption proved to be very far from the case. A committee of the three organisations including ten councillors had agreed in 1768 that a fourth church was needed but thereafter the town council ignored all communications from the session. Increasingly exasperated the session decided in July 1771 that they would take silence as refusal and asked the

Trades if they would be prepared to go ahead without town council help.[21] After receiving satisfactory answers to their various questions regarding the eventual control of the church, which they wanted to be free of all town council influence, the Nine Trades agreed to contribute, providing the United Trades would take their share.[22] The new church was expected to provide a place of worship for the poor in the town and a public appeal was made. By April 1772 a long list of subscriptions had been collected including £1.11s.6d. from an Amsterdam man and £30 from the duke of Atholl.[23]

The architect was the Dundonian, Samuel Bell, and estimates of local tradesmen were accepted for the masonry, slating and wright work: £546 from David Beath or Boath the mason, £745 from Thomas Baillie and £115 from the slater, William Law. They were all members of the relevant United Trades and Bell himself was a master wright. In fact the costs rose between £400 and £500 but these were accepted and in 1775 St Andrew's, a notable addition to Dundee's townscape, was ready for worship.

Though the kirk session of the parish churches and the Trades were joint owners of the fabric of the church and of the ground on which it was built, and received a regular income from the congregation, interest on the money they had laid out, a committee of the congregation carried out the day-to-day management. This caused some disagreements as the Trades did not always want to see more money spent, though they had agreed to build a house for meetings of St Andrew's kirk session in 1776.[24] There was also annoyance in 1796 when the Trades realised that the account books of St Andrews were being audited only by the town churches' kirk session, though they had an equal interest in the church's finances.[25]

The fact that as owners the Trades and kirk session shared the patronage of the new kirk, that is the power to call a minister to the charge, led to controversy between the two bodies. A selection committee of 20 members of the session, 15 representatives of the Nine and five of the United Trades met to make a choice. Congregations were excluded from any say in choosing their pastors in the Church of Scotland, and resentment about this was one of the causes of the Disruption of 1843 when the Free Church was founded by those who were unhappy about this and other aspects of the established church.

Trouble erupted between Trades and St Andrew's kirk session in 1806 when it was necessary to find a replacement for Rev. Thomas Rait, the first incumbent of St Andrew's. Some more evangelically-minded members of the kirk session, notably Rev. Mr Davidson, wanted to lessen the Trades' influence, particularly concerning the choice of a pastor. Not all the Nine

Trades had been happy about having a share in building the new church with accompanying responsibility as its proprietors thereafter. The Bonnetmakers who had initially 'declined any connection' with the new church[26] seized the opportunity to sell their share to the session, as did the Dyers. This would have given the kirk session a controlling vote in any decisions made about St Andrew's.

The Nine Trades sought the opinion of counsel as to whether this was legal and took their case to the Court of Session. However, a group in the kirk session supported their case and none was very keen on litigation. By May 1807 the kirk session was making advances to the Trades to settle their differences.[27] It was agreed that the Bonnetmakers and Dyers could buy back their shares, though if they refused the Nine Trades would take them. The session and the Trades were to choose a minister alternately. On the first occasion on which this compromise was to operate, a lottery was to decide which body should exercise the privilege. The session won, a waiter at the hotel where the meeting was held having carried out the draw.[28]

The Trades remained proprietors of the church until late in 1872. Before that time they had had to help cope with many problems that arose. One ordained minister, Mr MacNeil, became mentally ill but survived for over thirty years, confined to an institution. His stipend, however, had still to be paid and they also had to provide for temporary replacements. They also found themselves supporting a school started by Mr Ewing the church's highly respected evangelical minister. Many of the congregation had refused to pay their seat rents in April 1843 as they were uncertain that he would remain their pastor when the expected Disruption occurred.

Mr Ewing did in fact join the Free Church and questions, large and small, were inevitably raised thereafter regarding all aspects of the management of the church. Even the ownership of the church's library which had been removed was a problem – did it belong to the proprietors or the subscribers? It was also proposed that members of the Nine Trades who had left the established church should resign from a committee of the Trades which managed a building that adhered to it. One did but others staunchly refused to do so. A row within the Nine Trades also broke out over the appointment of counsel by a joint committee of proprietors before the Disruption to advise them on the legality of various steps taken about the church. Some members alleged that this had been done by a small group preparing to secede and thought his fee should not be paid.[29]

By the 1860s it would seem that the Trades were beginning to draw away from such a close connection with the church. In 1864 they objected to any increase in the stipend, saying the kirk session had more interest in the church than the Trades and they should arrange any augmentation.[30] They resolved to take no part in appointing a new minister. St Andrew's had never been part of the establishment of the town kirks and in 1869 when the suggestion was made that it should, the Trades wondered if a change of proprietors was perhaps in order. When the decision to sell was taken in 1871, only one person dissented[31] and the Dundee Presbytery duly bought out the twelve Trades for £200.

However, St Andrew's and the Trades are still bound by history and sentiment. The minister of the church is the Trades' chaplain, and is usually made an honorary member. The Trades meet in the old Glasite church which is now the session house before their annual 'kirking'. Pews in the front of the gallery, widened for comfort in 1867, are the Trades'; in 1874 emblems of each Trade were put on the deacons' chairs.[32] The Trades have never lost their interest in the building itself. The Trades keep their own bibles in the church, the deacon-convener's chair remains there. Stained-glass windows were installed to celebrate the church's centenary of 1887 at the suggestion of Rev. Mr Davidson, the incumbent at the time,[33] though they were not installed until 1892. The Nine Trades were responsible for two large windows displaying the Trades' emblems on either side of the pulpit and the United Trades for two smaller emblems. Some of the Trades' old banners or flags are exhibited in the building and the gallery was decorated with two plaques in 1962, one bearing the arms of the Nine, the other that of the three United Trades.

NOTES

[1] NT4.1.

[2] DDARC, GD/TD/W2.2, 4.11.1828.

[3] DDL, GLB.

[4] DDARC, GD/TD/W2.2, 4.5.1830.

[5] DDARC, GD/TD/T1.1, 13, 15.8.1816.

[6] NT2.7, 16.9.1834.

[7] DDARC, GD/TD/T5.16, 25.12.1759.

[8] DDARC, GD/TD/T.22–23.

[9] DDARC, GD/TD/W2.2, 2.3.1836.

[10] DDARC, GD/TD/T5.43.

[11] DDARC, GD/TD/W2.2, 19.3.1841.

[12] NT2.6, 4.1.1841.

[13] DDARC, GD/TD/T1.3, 15.1.1841; 4.8.1841.

[14] DDARC, GD/TD/T1.4, 19.2.1842.

[15] DDARC, GD/TD/T1.5, 25.9.1843.

[16] DDARC, GD/TD/T1.4, p. 17.

[17] DDARC, GD/TD/T1.4, 29.1.1844; 13.3.1844.

[18] DDARC, GD/TD/T1.5, 9.12.1873.

[19] NT2.5, 26.11.1801.

[20] NT4.1, p. 9, 1698–99.

[21] NT2.5, 21.5.1771.

[22] Smith, 1987, 37–38.

[23] NT5.13.

[24] NT2.5, 29.2.1776.

[25] Ibid., 19.10.1796.

[26] Ibid., 26.5.1774.

[27] Ibid., 20.5.1807

[28] Smith, 1987, 40.

[29] NT2.6, 1843, *passim*.

[30] NT2.1, December 1864.

[31] Ibid., 8.3.1871.

[32] Ibid., 26.1.1874.

[33] Ibid., 2.3.1887.

The Trades Hall

For centuries the usual meeting place of the nine incorporations had been in some area in the town churches, sometimes the vestry. After Mary Queen of Scots gave the town the gift of the land that had belonged to the Greyfriars to be used as a burial ground, general meetings of the Trades were almost always held there in the 'sepulchre'. As a result it became known as the Howff, sometimes holf in the Trades' records, a meeting place. Each Trade had its own meeting place too, usually the gravestone of one of its former members. Meetings called by the Collector and later the Deacon-convener first met 'in common hall' at the Nine Trades' general meeting place and then the Trades departed to decide separately how they would vote on the various issues under discussion. A stone still standing in the Howff has been identified as the gathering place of the 'haill trades', the description often given to them in the records and a picture of this is to be found among the illustrations.

The gate of the graveyard seems to have been under lock and key for the accounts show payment to the 'keeper of the sepulchre door' 4s. – for opening it to the Trades – though sometimes the grave-diggers were so employed.[1] The Howff cannot always have been the most comfortable place for serious discussion though no suggestion has been found that their rendezvous should be changed until 1776. In June of the previous year, the Trades heard that the flesh shambles and a house at the head of the Murraygate were for sale. Looking at this as initially simply an advantageous purchase to help their poor fund, the General Fund Court decided to bid for it.

Their bid of £351 plus £40 for ten foot more ground on the west end of the tenement was successful. It is possible that some members were being devious about their plans, for no mention of using the site for building a hall for themselves was made in the minutes when the matter was mentioned. It will be remembered that this is the period when the Convener Court's methods were less than open. By the time it came to reporting the purchase to the whole Trades in March 1776 it must be assumed that discussion had been taking place at some depth outside formal meetings.[2] Otherwise it would probably have been impossible to obtain the comprehensive agreement that was arrived at in one meeting. Of course it has to be remembered that this is the period described by the committee which produced the 1819 constitution as being 'buried in darkness'.

It was decided at the March meeting that the shambles should be demolished after Whit – there would be tacks of part of it to be honoured. On the site the Trades should build as many shops as possible at ground level, and

2. STONE IN THE HOWFF, WHERE THE 'HAILL TRADES' MET

(Spanphoto, Dundee)

a large hall above, with small rooms leading off it for the use of the individual Trades. The building was to be the property of the General Fund Court.

By the middle of April estimates had been received from a mason, Walter Bain, for £666. James Barrie and Ninian Alexander offered £596 for wright work and James Nicoll £519.16s. for slating. Samuel Bell was the architect and his final account came to £42.10s. By March 1778 the hall was ready for plastering and this time craftsmen from Cupar in Fife, Robert Hamilton and Alex Duncan, were employed, being deemed the best in the country. Their bill was £51.19s.11d. In the summer the shops were being leased, and some merchants proposed that they should hire the hall as a coffee house.

The rooms off the hall which each Trade was to have for its own use were ready in August and lots were drawn to decide which each should have. The lottery was not indiscriminate; the smaller incorporations, Glovers, Bonnetmakers, Fleshers and Waulkers drew for the smaller rooms. The General Fund Court was to be allowed to let the large hall and two smaller rooms were divided with a removable partition. At the meeting held in the Howff, on 23 September 1778, the deacon-convener proposed that they should meet in the hall the next day for the elections. The following day they assembled in the ancient graveyard and from there marched proudly to the new Trades Hall. Later they processed to St Andrew's church to attend a service there. Convener Bisset led the procession, wearing the new gold chain and medal which the Nine Trades had just commissioned. Then came the deacons carrying their Trade's flags followed by the rest of the members of the Nine. They did not meet again in the Howff until 1991 when Dundee was celebrating 800 years as a Royal Burgh and the whole Nine Trades repeated the walk from the Howff, on this occasion to a service of celebration and thanksgiving in St Andrew's.

The hall was clearly not completely ready for comfortable use in September despite being used as a coffee house. In December the convener was authorised to buy two carron grates with fenders, poker and tongs as well as material for curtains and blinds. After the initial euphoria reality set in; the Trades found themselves facing continual calls on the funds for upkeep and maintenance, not unusual in a large building. Slate work was needed by 1781 and by 1815 reroofing was necessary which cost £130.10s.[3] In 1792 David Thomson, a wright, offered £15 to repair the cupola where the bell hung and keep it in good order for seven years at £1 per annum.[4] In June 1822 the outside wall was described as 'going fast into decay' and by August almost £100 had been spent on repairs.[5] Gas was installed in 1826, on the initiative of the tenants of the Coffee House who offered to furnish burners.

The original costs had also turned out to be larger than the estimates. In 1780 the convener had to remind the Nine that a considerable sum was still owing on 'the large tenement at the head of the Murraygate and Seagate commonly called the Trades Hall'. It had been agreed that an extra 2d. should be paid on each boll of meal bought by each Trade but that was not nearly enough. He proposed that an extra 5s. should be paid by each new master and 5s. in addition to the marriage merk, while apprentices should be asked for 5s. The Trades all agreed to the extra imposition.[6]

The 19 year leases of the shops were due to be renewed in 1805–6 and the negotiations aroused some concern among members when the convener let one to himself in partnership with another tenant. The Trades decided to prosecute him and a court case resulted which the Trades lost but an amicable settlement was eventually reached by February 1806.[7] The premises were all let by public roup at the end of each tack.

The Exchange Coffee House was successful for many years, but sometimes tried to negotiate a reduction in its rent when takings were down by threatening to move. In March 1828 the Trades heard a rumour that the coffee room subscribers were collecting funds to build their own hall as they believed the Trades offered only an annual lease to enable them to raise the rent regularly.[8] Rather anxiously the Nine Trades offered a ten year tack, for the let was worth £70 to £80. They had always retained the right to use the large hall for their Michaelmas and other General Meetings on Sundays from 10 a.m. to 4 p.m. and some members wondered if this made the tenancy less attractive.

The rumour was of course correct. In 1828–29 the Exchange Coffee House was commissioned, designed by George Smith. This building now houses Winter's stationery business.[9] Having lost such lucrative regular tenants the Trades decided to keep the hall on as a coffee shop but with their rules operating and then as a reading room. Only the Bakers supported it in sufficient numbers to have made it profitable. Others did not even pay their subscriptions, though these had been set at only 10s. to 12s. Perhaps there was not room for two competing coffee houses in Dundee at the time.[10]

The accommodation in the building was never fully used by the Trades themselves. The small rooms were often let or used for committee meetings. The Weavers had allowed both flaxdressers and hecklers to meet in their room in 1789, charging 2s. to the first and 10s. to the second group.[11] The main hall was used often by other public bodies as well as for general meetings of the Nine Trades. As early as 1784 it had been let for the month of July to a group for presenting plays.[12] The Guildry and burgesses held a dinner there in October 1820 and in 1833 it housed the *usual* exhibition of the Horticultural Society. In June 1833 a Mr Springthorpe offered £10 a month for three months for a waxworks exhibition but the Trades felt there might be difficulties in persuading the subscribers to the coffee room to give up their meeting place for such a purpose. There was also a suggestion that it might be used as a theatre.

By the 1830s the building was showing worrying signs of dilapidation. Over £50 had to be spent on repairs in 1834. Holes in the front had to be filled with cement, the ornamental parts were a danger to the public, particularly the central vase, and the pavement required lowering all round to correspond with the new causeway.[13] The General Fund Court, responsible for the Hall, must have been very relieved to be approached by the new Eastern Bank of Scotland asking if they could lease the hall and rooms.[14]

Each Trade's consent to giving up its room had to be obtained. There were complications caused by the rights of tenants and subtenants of the individual Trades' rooms and by the existence of the shops let below, but agreement was reached. The bank took over the property at a rent of £140 p.a. and all the furniture belonging to the Trades was sold in June 1838.[15] Each Trade received compensation in rent for the loss of the use of its room.

The bank expressed a preference later in 1838 for either a longer lease than that originally granted or the option of buying the whole property. They argued that they needed to spend hundreds of pounds on heating. The figures of £6,000, £7,000 and £8,000 appeared but a longer lease was agreed by November 1839. The Trades Hall was inhabited by a bank for the rest of its existence.

The Trades as owners were still responsible for the outside fabric of the hall and in 1850 began extensive improvements to the shops on street level, including more modern windows. During the alterations a brass plate was found inscribed with the names of the convener and deacons in office in 1775 on one side and on the other the information that the plate had been laid by the master of St David's Lodge, George Patterson, Esq. A new one was ordered with the names of the present committee of the General Fund Court, convener and deacons. Money had to be borrowed to pay for all the changes costing £770.12s. All the shop tenants had been asked to leave and when the alterations were complete, J.H. Lawrie, a draper in Reform Street, rented all the premises at ground level.

The need for more repairs arose in 1863 and in February 1864 the Trades authorised the sale of the hall they had entered so hopefully in 1778. The Clydesdale Bank was the purchaser as it had taken over the Eastern Bank in 1863. Each Trade received compensation for the loss of rent from its room and the sale brought the General Fund over £6,000.[16] The bell from the cupola was kept for sentiment's sake 'as a relic' and the Directors of the bank offered to restore it, preparatory to its being placed in the spire of the Town House.[17] Throughout the years of the bank's tenancy access had been allowed to the cupola to ring the 'fine-toned' bell on public occasions.

In 1876 to assist town council improvement schemes the Trades Hall was demolished. It took up too much space, causing congestion at the end of the Murraygate and Seagate. Its replacement still stands there, the triangular Clydesdale Bank, designed by William Spence, which has been described as 'dully Renaissance' and much less pleasant than the Trades Hall.[18]

NOTES

[1] NT4.1, 1705.

[2] NT2.5, 12.3.1776.

[3] Ibid., 24.6.1815.

[4] Ibid., 15.8.1792.

[5] Ibid., 9.8.1822.

[6] Ibid., 11.9.1780.

[7] Ibid., 5.2.1806.

[8] NT2.6, 21.3.1828.

[9] David M. Walker, *Dundee Architecture and Architects*, Abertay Historical Society Publication No. 18 (Dundee, 1977), 9. Hereafter Walker, 1977.

[10] NT2.6, 13.2.1832.

[11] DDARC, GD/TD/W3.1.

[12] NT1.1.

[13] NT2.7, August, December 1834.

[14] Ibid., 23.5.1838.

[15] Ibid., 4.6.1838.

[16] NT2.1, 8.9.1870.

[17] NT2.7, 5.7.1865.

[18] Walker, 1977, 23.

The Trades and the Town Council

Relations between the Trades and the town council were marked by tension throughout much of their history as long as the Trades had legal privileges to guard jealously. This is not to be wondered at. The deacons of the Trades took part in the election of the provost and magistrates by long-established right. Under the conditions laid down in the old set of the burgh, which was in force until 1818, the convener of the Nine Trades was given leets for the provost, treasurer and bailies which the Trades voted on. The deacons then joined the old and new councils in electing these officials. In 1696 the Convener reminded the tradesmen that by an act of the parliament of Scotland those who did not exercise their vote would lose it.[1]

By 1554 a craftsman was the keeper of the key of one of the three locks which secured the town's kist.[2] As this chest contained all the charters and other important documents belonging to Dundee, it demonstrates the pre-eminent place of the crafts in the burgh. The craftsmen were so sure of this that in 1563 the keeper of the third key, Alexander Carnegy, refused to open the kist to allow the common seal of the burgh to be attached to the commission of the council to two members to attend a meeting of parliament.[3] His reason for this contumacy was that the Trades had forbidden him to do so as there were no craftsmen members on the commission. The council claimed this was a 'novation' which may be so as the craftsmen apparently bore no direct share in members' expenses.

The craftsmen believed they were due a share in the administration but the town council resented this claim and resisted it as far as they could. The areas which at a later date caused particular animosity were the calling of ministers to the town kirks, the appointment of the main council officials, particularly the town clerk, and the rights of the Trades to approve the financial dealings of the council. In addition the Trades made it quite clear to those of their number who sat on the council that they must at all times defend the interests of the Trades and vote according to the Trades' instructions.[4]

From the time of James II until the beginning of the seventeenth century the Trades had had two representatives on the council, the Trades councillors; the Guildry had ten. All the deacons attended what was sometimes described as Grand Council meetings. Some acts of the council to which the deacons were party which concern the craftsmen are to be found in the Collector's Book which dates from 1568.[5] In 1568 the deacons were present protesting in the name of all the masters of the burgh that there should be no 'novations' without the advice of all of them. In September 1573 the collector and deacons were among those passing ordinances referring to all writs in the common kist, the town's chest, which concerned them, and to various financial arrangements. This was a pattern of interest which was to last throughout the Trades' history as long as they had privileges to defend though the Trades had no representation on the council after 1833.

By the beginning of the seventeenth century the Trades felt they merited more representation on the council. They were encouraged by one of the bailies, Robert Flesher, and by Reverend Robert Howie, minister on the first charge in the town churches. Howie was a rumbustious character whose support did not tend to conciliation. The Trades' claims became mixed up with discontent over the position of the provost, Sir James Scrymgeour, who was also constable of the burgh. This conjunction of posts had never been popular with the townspeople. There were riots, bakers deposed their deacon and were imprisoned, with Mr Howie undertaking their defence paid by their wives. The Synod of Angus and the Privy Council were involved, the Privy Council restoring the Baxter Trade's deacon, and an appeal was also made by the Crafts to the Convention of Royal Burghs. Howie tried without success to influence the Convention by going with several hundred supporters to Perth where the commissioners were meeting.[6]

The Trades not unnaturally disagreed with the decision of the Convention's decreet which did not actually state the number of craftsmen who should be on the council. On 19 September 1604 the collector, Robert Goldman, appeared before the council to defend their previous behaviour and to request that they should have four members, chosen from collector and deacons. A rival council was elected by the disaffected members but does not seem to have lasted long. The collector and deacons were all deposed in March 1605 by royal edict and their predecessors installed in their places. Noisy and insulting objections resulted in more craftsmen being imprisoned. Later in the year on 23 September, William Goldman, dean of Guild, objected to there being four craftsmen on the council but a compromise was reached the following year that there should be three.[7] Three craftsmen sat on the council thereafter until the nineteenth century when more changes took place.

There was general dissatisfaction with both burgh and parliamentary franchise in the late eighteenth and early nineteenth centuries. In Dundee the Guildry became restless that their dean was elected by the town council and had been since the council arrogated this power to themselves in 1605. The Trades assisted the Guildry in this fight, making the interesting point that they had sanctioned the removal of this right and wondered why they had not been called on to join in its repeal. On 16 July 1818 the Convention of Royal Burghs responded to a petition from council, magistrates, the Nine Trades, the Guildry and burgesses of Dundee by changing the set of the burgh. The convener, elected by the Trades, was to be an *ex officio* member of the council, two places still to be filled by other craftsmen. The Guildry regained their power to elect their dean of Guild who also sat as an *ex officio* councillor.[8]

In 1830 the burgh was temporarily disfranchised but an Order in Council in 1831 put in place a temporary set in which the council was elected by rate-paying burgesses. The convener of the Trades and the dean of Guild were both members.[9] Two years later, however, the Burgh Reform Act[10] was passed and the Trades lost their place for ever, though the dean of Guild retained his. The omission of the convener as a member seems to have been accidental but despite assistance from trade incorporations in other Scottish towns, it proved impossible to reinstate the Trades' representative.[11]

Apart from representation on the council there was no doubt historically about the participation of the Nine Trades in burgh management; town council records themselves illustrate this. On 10 December 1607 prices were fixed 'with consent of deacons of crafts', a pint of ale to be not dearer than 10d., an 18 ounce loaf of wheat bread to cost 12d. In January 1651 the council agreed to the crafts' request that Sir Alexander Wedderburn be restored to the position of town clerk. The deacons took part with the council in February 1700 in choosing a new minister.[12]

The pressing economic problems of the burgh at the end of the seventeenth century were partly responsible for bringing latent hostility between council and craftsmen into the open but the Trades were bound to be somewhat ambiguous in their attitude to the council. As early as 1628 they complained about irregularities in the election of magistrates.[13] In 1676 at the Head Court they requested that their privileges should be renewed.[14] This and the appeal of some of the incorporations to the council for a change in their ranking in 1695[15] undoubtedly showed that they recognised that they were to some extent dependants of the town council, even though they used the earlier occasion to include a complaint about the state of the harbour. This was not the last expression of their doubts about the council's handling of the town's affairs.

At the beginning of May 1698 the convener and deacons protested strongly to the council on behalf of themselves, the Trades and 'other good burgesses' about what they saw as mismanagement if not abuse of the common good.[16] They claimed the town was 'drowned in debt' and their long list of grievances ranged from objections to money from the town's funds being spent on drinking and feasting in such circumstances to larger queries about necessary repairs to the harbour – the perennial worry – and the need to see accounts regarding the town's purchase of the barony of the Hilltown.

In what was probably an attempt to ward off any more criticism the town council agreed with the Trades on 31 May and 2 June that in future the deacon-convener should audit all public accounts and those of the common good except those of the Guildry. Despite this agreement and although the protest had been copied into the convener's book 'for a pattern and example to posterity' to show the part of the Trades in trying to preserve the town's credit, it is plain the council did not mend its ways immediately. At the election in September the Trades planned to try to change the membership of the council.[17] One of their lines of attack was that provost James Fletcher had been in office too long and it is interesting to find that he claimed at this point that he was not obliged to give an account of the common good to the king. Another attempt at compromise may have been the response to a petition from James Whyte, deacon-convener at the time; the 1560 ratification of the Trades' privileges was corroborated and the charter was laid in the convener's kist.[18]

Dundee's finances were in such a state in the first decade of the eighteenth century that in November the Trades reported that the magistrates had refused to accept appointment.[19] Another difficulty arose when during Head Court meetings two or three magistrates passed acts which the Trades decided to ignore 'when they fell on their way'.[20] The Trades went to law against the magistrates to prevent 'intrusion on their privileges' and on 18 April 1710 the council reacted with a frontal attack on the Trades.

The council claimed the Trades' only powers were to appoint a deacon who could regulate the work of his own craft but any fines were to be determined by the magistrates. The crunch of the battle was the fees some of the incorporations 'extravagantly exact' from the unfree. According to the town this was probably the reason for the town being so depopulated, with houses in decay. This charge the Trades of course vehemently denied. To correct the position the council fixed 50 merks as the entry fee of unfree as well as imposing set figures for other normal exaction. The Trades decided to go to the Court of Session to defend what they considered their undoubted liberties and a long battle ensued.[21]

Charges and counter-charges and insults followed. Individual Trades were named for particular 'abuses'. The worst attack perhaps was on the competence of the Cordiners and Tailors who were accused of being such poor workmen that Dundonians had to go elsewhere to buy shoes and clothes. Unfortunately, none of the Trades seemed to be able to produce their Seals of Cause. In December 1712 the Lords of Session found that while the Trades could make laws for their respective incorporations for ordinary management, the magistrates of the town had a power to review their bye-laws and regulations.

One of the side effects of the case was that the council decided that the magistrates could intervene if a deacon declared a would-be master incapable, and could call on tradesmen from other burghs to assess the applicant's work.[22] The craftsmen must have been very dissatisfied with the outcome and even more unhappy when faced with the bill. It had been agreed that the General Fund could legitimately be called on to cover the costs of the case but in 1717 each Trade had to find £54 to repay this.[23]

As they could no longer exact higher fees from incoming masters, in order to increase their funds, usually on the grounds that more was needed for the poor fund, the Trades simply increased the 'accidents' that new masters and apprentices had to pay. In 1724 the Dyers for example commented that the decay in trade 'incapacitated' them from giving the poor all they needed. They lengthened apprenticeships to six years plus two as servant and asked for £5 for entry, 1d. for use of the mortcloth and £10 instead of the dinner and accidents. They also refused all credit.[24]

In 1735 the town council was asked for permission to raise the entry fees. The Trades argued that the circumstances of the burgh had altered so much that now too many unfree were entering the burgh and craftsmen were having great difficulty in earning their living. The Head Court endorsed the council's agreement on 5 January 1736 but it included the proviso that the increased entry fee should be all that was asked for booking money. This removed the flexibility the Trades had been exercising in their financial affairs and the convener and deacons immediately objected but without apparent effect.[25] A further row erupted in the 1750s which once again went to the Court of Session and was not finally settled until 1766. During these years the council made the extraordinary statement that they did not know what a Seal of Cause was. The Trades felt with some reason that they were being elbowed out of their position vis-à-vis the council. At one point they asserted that their rights were being assailed because the magistrates and council were almost entirely merchants and guild brethren. The council wavered in its behaviour; in February 1761 there was a comment on their having retracted from such agreement as appeared to have been reached. The Court of Session eventually decided that the Trades had no place in appointing the town's ministers but confirmed other claims.

Town property could not be sold, let or feued without their participation in the process and they could vote in electing the town clerk.[26]

In the following years for a time the town council was fairly circumspect in ensuring that the Trades were consulted on matters where their rights were now legally acknowledged. The court case must have been expensive for town as well as Trades and there was always the fact that the Trades could and sometimes did refuse to sign bonds if they felt ignored. It was an uneasy truce which was unlikely to last and when faced with the general movement for political reform of burghs and parliament, wholeheartedly embraced by the Trades and equally wholeheartedly opposed by councillors who could see only loss for themselves in change, it finally broke down.

The craftsmen's enthusiastic approval for the 'spirit of liberty' was expressed in 1783.[27] In the following years funds were readily made available to forward the cause of reform including the expense of sending a delegate to conventions on electoral reform. The excesses of the French Revolution killed the prospect of general reform until the next century but the Trades did not forget their crusade for a more liberal constitution.

One aspect of the council's management of elections particularly incensed the incorporations. In October 1789 the managers of the General fund pointed out that the 'so-called Trades Councillors' were elected by the council and had not voted with the Trades at the election of magistrates for sometime. It was decided not to call them to meetings in future.[28] According to the Trades, the council had elected only craftsmen in 1818, under the new set, whom they knew they could control and in addition on one occasion at least had chosen men from only one Trade, which was not desirable from the Trades' viewpoint.[29]

A ridiculous situation arose in 1829. The convener reported to the Nine Trades that the council had accepted him but with objections and then elected him convener.[30] Needless to say the Trades were furious and instructed him to sit as the Trades' choice. Apart from anything else such behaviour was illegal according to the 1818 constitution and helps explain the suspension of the town council the following year.

Dundonians' desire for more say in the government of their town was being expressed very clearly in the campaigns for rights and reforms in the early years of the nineteenth century. Various groups in the town, not normally allies, co-operated for instance in trying to wrest power from the council when a Harbour Bill was going through parliament. Guildry and merchants not on the council were as active as any. The Trades managed to win places for three commissioners on the Harbour Board, which they retained until 1952.[31] There was great interest throughout the nineteenth century in all changes to the harbour. The representatives had to report back to the Trades until they decided that as the newspapers gave full reports the meetings held specially for that purpose could be given up.

All Scottish burgh councils could be described as 'self-perpetuating oligarchies' until 1833 except Dundee, where the council was elected by burgesses after 1831. This situation attracted more and more resentment, especially when it was felt, rightly or wrongly, that town funds were being used mainly to line the pockets of the men in power. The Trades had shown their desire for reform in the 1780s and their records in the years after Waterloo are full of criticisms of Dundee's council.

The language is hardly temperate. One provost was described as 'either under the management of Alexander Riddoch or else to be possessed of a mind so imbecile and wavering as to render him a most unfit person for holding office as the first magistrate of Dundee'.[32] The comment on Riddoch shows that the Trades were among those who supported the opponents of that 'artful and ambitious individual', who had been dominant in Dundee's affairs since he entered the council in 1776. In the eyes of would-be reformers he was the personification of all the evils they deplored in burgh government and his career has had to wait until late in this century for a more balanced assessment.[33]

The Trades' commitment to reform, both burgh and parliamentary cannot be doubted. They petitioned both Lords and Commons in 1831 for reform of the franchise and in 1867 considered another petition in favour of increased Scottish representation, particularly another member for Dundee. Their idealism, like that of many others, may not have been wholly altruistic but they were prepared to pay to support it and there can be no doubt that they were truly concerned about the welfare of the town and considered reform of the electoral system one way of improving its management.

Such attitudes clearly would not endear them to the group controlling the council, even though in fact they were not really able to influence decisions. If the twenty councillors were in agreement on financial matters, the votes of nine deacons were ineffective. The removal of any craft representation on the council in 1833 removed much of the acerbity from their relations with the town council. Once the Royal Burghs and incorporated Trades lost their peculiar privileges the areas of possible conflict were still further reduced though individual craftsmen could join the political fray on their own behalf.

The Nine Trades' long-established place in the fabric of Dundee society ensured a practical place for them long after the loss of their official position on the council. Assisting with harbour management was only one of these areas where their influence was still felt. The lunatic asylum was another, while Trades and town worked together to ensure that the Morgan bequest was retained by the town.[34] On the other hand they felt any action to obtain better lighting on the Tay was better left to Trinity House.[35] Public ceremonies such as meeting Queen Victoria in 1844, or the opening of the Baxter Park in 1863, were graced by their presence though on occasion individual Trades decided to march with their masonic lodges instead of their own Trade. During the Crimean War they were incensed when they heard a rumour that the council had refused to accept guns offered by the government for the defence of the Tay. A special General Meeting was called to overturn this decision. The rumour turned out to be false but once again the Trades had demonstrated that they looked on anything that might affect the town as rightly their concern.

In these days of universal franchise in both town and parliamentary elections, the battles that helped to win these rights have become a distant memory. It is unlikely that later generations of town councillors and craftsmen ever give a thought to or even know of the strife that caused so much expense and anxiety to their forebears. The one thing that is certain is that the Nine Trades are still as interested in the welfare of Dundee as they ever were.

NOTES

[1] NT4.1, 3.10.1696.

[2] Maxwell, *The History of Old Dundee* (1884), 33. Hereafter Maxwell, 1884.

[3] Ibid., 184–185.

[4] NT2.3, 29.9.1628.

[5] Ibid.

[6] See Maxwell, 1884, 353–368 for a detailed description of this disagreement.

[7] NT5.2a.

[8] CLB2; NT2.5, 25.9.1817; *Dundee, Perth and Cupar Advertiser*, 14.8.1818.

[9] Whatley, 1993, 134.

[10] 9 Vic. c. 17.

[11] NT2.6, 9.10.1833; 2.7.1833; 1834 *passim*.

[12] NT5.2.

[13] NT2.3, 29.9.1628.

[14] Warden, 1872, 258.

[15] See Chapter 1.

[16] NT4.1, 2.5.1698.

[17] Ibid., 27.9.1698.

[18] Ibid., 7.11.1699.

[19] Ibid., November 1705.

[20] Ibid.

[21] NT5.2. All the papers relating to this case are contained in this file.

[22] NT5.2, 13.11.1713.

[23] NT1.7, 5.2.1717.

[24] DLB, 11.9.1724.

[25] NT5.7.

[26] NT5.3. for papers referring to this case. Also mentioned in 5.2a.

[27] NT2.5, 24.2.1783.

[28] NT2.3, 6.10.1789.

[29] NT2.5, 5.10.1818.

[30] NT2.6, 23.9.1829.

[31] NT2.2, 2.2.1952.

[32] NT2.5, 23.9.1819.

[33] Enid Gauldie, *One Artful and Ambitious Individual*, Abertay Historical Society Publication No. 28 (Dundee, 1989). Hereafter Gauldie, 1989.

[34] NT2.6, 12.5.1858.

[35] Ibid., December 1867.

3. THE TRADES HALL

(The *Courier*, Dundee)

CHAPTER 4

The Baker Trade – The Baxters

The incorporated Baker Trade stands first among the Nine Trades. Until the middle of the eighteenth century the Craft kept the name of Baxter, Scots for baker. In 1768 both baxter and baker can be found on the same page in the Lockit Book but by the mid-1770s, the anglicised 'baker' had usurped the old name.[1]

Legal niceties apart, the Trade's pre-eminence is not surprising for bread was the most important food, the 'staff of life', for most western Europeans until the American potato usurped it in some areas. Indeed, it is only in the later part of this century that increasing affluence and the availability of a greater choice of carbohydrates have displaced bread as the main 'filler' for all but the wealthiest.

The Bakers' charter which might have given documentary proof that the Baxters were the first Dundee trade to be incorporated has disappeared. A.J. Warden in 1872 shows no signs of having seen it, but the historian Alexander Maxwell in his book *Old Dundee. Ecclesiastical, Burghal and Social, prior to the Reformation* published in 1891 described a charter of 1486.[2] In this document the Craft was empowered to endow an altar in praise of St Cuthbert, the patron saint of bakers everywhere. The provost and town council undertook to ensure that the gifts bought for this altar were 'maintained' and 'defended', thereby clearly endorsing the Craft.

As the endowment of an altar and the promise to maintain a chaplain to say mass there were the usual means by which the Dundee Trades obtained recognition and permission to make their own rules and elect a deacon, it is more than likely that this document was the Baxters' Seal of Cause. It is the earliest on record in Dundee and could thus help to explain the pre-eminence of the Trade among the Nine. The 'letters' granted to the Trade by the provost, bailies and council are mentioned in what must have been the first entry in the new book of 1554,[3] though rebinding has misplaced it. Unfortunately the date of the letters is not mentioned. This entry of 23 November of that year gives the names and duties of 'assessors and examinators' who are to keep order and rule everything pertaining to their craft, conforming at the same time to the 'common weil'. In other words their private regulations must not clash with the laws of the burgh or the realm.

At that time the Bakers must have been a fairly wealthy group. No other member of the Nine Trades made such rich gifts to the altars they endowed; at least none were listed in the charters whose wording is known. The Bakers bought from Thomas Turnour of St Johnston (Perth) a mass book, newly written and bound, a silver chalice, vestments of silk and bukkasy (fine buckram) and chandeliers. These goods were to be kept solely for the upkeep of the altar, neither the chaplain nor anyone else ever to be allowed for any reason – for 'nae kind of necessity' – to sell or use them as security. The Trade was to choose the chaplain annually, each baker paying his weekly 'Cuthbert pennies' towards the upkeep of altar and custodian.

If a Lockit Book was bought at that time, it too has disappeared and the Baker Trade's extant records begin in 1554 with a book which continued in use until 1778. Its successor was replaced in 1988 through the generosity of the heirs of a former deacon, Fred Brown, who died before he could carry out his offer to buy the Trade a new book. It had been estimated in 1984 that a new Lockit Book would be needed in two or three years time at a cost of £500 and without this gift the Bakers might not now possess quite such a handsome volume as they currently use.[4]

As in other Lockit Books that have been rebound, entries have been misplaced. What contemporary brethren described in 1554 as 'The common buyk' of the craft now opens with much later entries. The first, just inside the cover, is an undated inventory of debts due to the Trade. Following this are two later decisions of the incorporation, made in 1687 and 1697, which will be considered later in connection with the business they dealt with. Next comes the date of the book and after two blank pages, the oath that all entrants had to subscribe to. This was of the usual form, demanding obedience to God, the king, the provost and bailies, and to the deacon and brethren of the craft. It was only his deacon and craft and its liberties, however, not king and country, that the new baker was asked to defend with his body and goods.

The oath was designed for apprentices and journeymen on their entry to the Trade as well as for masters; the fifth clause includes the need to be an obedient and true servant to the entrant's master as well as the injunction, common to many indentures, neither to hear or see any skaith – injury of any kind – to that master, or indeed to any member of the craft without trying to stop it. It remained substantially unaltered until the nineteenth century when in 1820 a new master promised only to discharge every civil duty incumbent by law on a freemaster and a member of the Baker Trade.[5]

After the original oath, the next two pages record what must originally have been the first entry. On 23 November 1554 in Greyfriars Kirk, there occurred the election of Alexander Browne as deacon, Johne Rob as officer, Sir Thomas Wedderburn as chaplain and the 'assessors and examinators', the deacon's advisory council, for the year to come. The most important members of the town council are listed, as well as 52 master bakers plus three at the foot of the page written in a different hand and ink. How many of these were actually present is uncertain but the list shows how large the Trade was. Thereafter, for 204 years this Lockit Book records elections of deacons, officers and assessors, the auditing of the deacons' accounts, the indenturing of apprentices, the entry of masters and the statutes and ordinances of the Trade. The Lockit Book does not however make any mention of the stirring events of the early 1600s when their deacon was deposed by the Trade and re-instated by the Scottish Privy Council.

Before the Howff was gifted to the town by Mary Queen of Scots in 1564, the trade met in various places, depending on the type of meeting. The election of deacons and a varying number of assessors, fourteen in 1554, ten in 1558, continued to be held in Greyfriars Kirk until that church was demolished by order of the town council in 1560.[6] Thereafter the Trade moved temporarily to Tenterhill for their main meetings but once the Howff was established as the usual gathering place for the Trades, the grave of a prominent family of Dundee bakers, the Tendalls, became their particular assembly point.[7] A deacon's accounts, however, seem regularly to have been examined in his own home and quite important meetings of the Trade were often held in private houses.[8]

The Howff cannot have been the warmest or driest place for meetings, especially when decisions of the Trades had to be recorded. On one occasion, 16 June 1621, after holding a court there and concluding their business – the level of apprentices' entry fees – the sensible bakers retired to James Fyf's dwelling where the new rules were written out by a Notary Public and witnessed by those brethren who had accompanied the lawyer.[9]

In the case of those trades who still possess their Seal of Cause or a copy of it, the wording usually indicates that the craftsmen had organised themselves into a private society to regulate the behaviour of members before they sought recognition from the town council. It would be very odd if such an important and wealthy group as the bakers had not in fact done so but so far we lack proof of such activity. There were certainly good professional bakers in the town. In the fourteenth century they are on record as having provided bread for the royal household on more than one occasion.[10]

From the first founding of royal burghs, the trade as a whole was exposed to pressures, national and burghal, that were almost bound to lead to co-operation among its members. One of the controls exercised by the burgh council by the authority of the Law of the Four Burghs was the fixing of the price of grain and meal, as well as malt, which also affected bakers as several brewed ale, the common drink for centuries, as well as baking bread.[11] The price and pais (the weight) of loaves was fixed by the town magistrates – the assize of bread. The council also made rules about the methods of baking, insisting for instance on well-sifted flour. The weight of loaves was supposed to depend on the price of wheat, and between November 1520 and October 1523 the council made six changes in the weight of loaves.[12]

Bakers did not always feel they were given a fair deal. One baker who was fined for selling underweight bread in the 1520s ended up with a further penalty, wax and candles for the mass, because he charged the officer with using false weights.[13] The harvest of 1522–23 was excellent and because of the low price of grain, bakers were ordered to cut the price of bread. They countered this by pointing out that fuel was scarce and the wheat was 'weak', not good for bread-making. Their plea was heeded on this occasion and they were allowed to charge two pence for 28 ounce loaves instead of the usual two pounder, 32 ounces.[14]

Working as a group bakers must have had more chance to bring the council round to their opinion but they did not always win the argument. Both council and Craft would have argued that they were trying to maintain good quality bread and a fair price for the lieges but they were looking at the question from different points of view. The council saw their duty as keeping the price of bread as low as possible for Dundonians, while the bakers had to protect their own livelihood. In 1559 the Trade pursued the council to the Court of Session to try to repeal the town magistrates' order that bread should have a fixed price. This could have been very difficult in an era when harvests varied greatly from one season to another without such opportunities as now exist of remedying shortages by imports or of exporting surpluses.

On occasion the bakers stopped or threatened to stop baking. After David Carnegy was fined for refusing to sell bread to the servants of bailie David Rollock in October 1557, there was a real crisis. The burgh was threatened with famine when the bakers did go on strike, specifically refusing to bake from noon on Saturday until Sunday evening. Each was fined 8s. and the council threatened offenders with banishment from the burgh for a year and a day. Even worse from the incorporation's point of view, it was suggested that unfree men would be licensed to bake if masters would not take an oath to observe the statutes on bread and ale. Feelings must have been running high for it was ten days before the Deacon and 45 master bakers appeared before the magistrates, took the oath and returned to their bakehouses.[15] In one year of scarcity, a few years later in 1562, the bakers were so unhappy about the council's decision that the deacon warned that the Trade would not supply bread at a price that threatened its liberties.[16]

The quality of the flour used, oaten or wheaten, was very important. On 22 July 1687 the deacon and masters commented that the wheat from one source, Alexander Williamson and his wife, had been so unsatisfactory that they forbade any of the Trade to buy from them in the future under threat of fines of 10 merks for the first breach of the rules and £10 Scots for the second. Their wording was that they had been 'so often wranged' by what the Williamsons had sold them, but they do not specify whether it was the quality or quantity of the wheat that was not dependable. Either could cause the bakers great problems.[17]

The fault did not always lie with the miller. In 1617 the bakers felt it incumbent on themselves to control both the quality and quantity of their produce. Because of the 'great inormities and wrangis' done by some of their 'neighbours', in fact some of their members, they agreed that a fine of £4 should be imposed on any who did not bake enough bread of good 'stuff'. They did mention obedience to the magistrates but insisted that no sour flour or any kind of something 'deid', (the 'something' being illegible but it was clearly undesirable), should be added to the bread.[18] At the same time they also insisted that the selling price should not be lower than the cost of production.

The need to control the quality of flour eventually led the Dundee Trade to lease mills where they could appoint a miller as tenant who would be responsible to them. In 1780 the Trade took the tack of the town's two mills on the Dighty burn and in November appointed a mill master to deal with the mill accounts.[19] As they purchased the tack (the lease) of Gray mills fifteen years later, presumably mill-management had not lost them money.[20]

Millers were not popular anywhere. Their customers were often sure that they received less flour than their grain should have yielded, but it was impossible to prove that they had been cheated. The uneasy relationship between customer and miller was aggravated by thirlage. Until 1799, the grain from large areas of land in Scotland was thirled to a particular mill;[21]

the farmer had no choice in where he had his grain ground. If he decided to take his custom elsewhere he still had to pay the miller his legal dues, multure, and most just put up with the situation, if unhappily. When thirlage was abolished, the Trade fixed the cost of grinding each boll of meal at their mills in place of the multure. When the Trade took over the Gray mills before the abolition of thirlage, they agreed to pay the sellers of the tack, the trustees of the merchant, William Badenoch, 2s. sterling for each boll of wheat ground, but the millmaster was to exact multures from those who objected to paying this sum.

The following year the Trade laid down rules for both the miller and the bakers using the mills. The millmaster had to find a cautioner and have his accounts inspected twice yearly at Martinmas and Whit, old style, with any surplus to be at the disposal of the Trade. There are no accounts available for us to know if any surplus in fact arose. One tenant was to hold town and Gray mills. Bakers were not allowed to give up their turn to have their grain ground to anyone else, and further could not have more than 24 bolls ground at one time. This rule would ensure that no craftsman could monopolise the miller's service.[22]

Some of the rules made about the flour the craftsmen should use and the customers they should supply are puzzling and today would be described as restrictive practices. What damage could have been done to the craft by baking burgesses' flour? This was forbidden in July 1666.[23] The Trade obviously felt very strongly about this particular practice for the order was repeated in 1726 when masters, apprentices and journeymen were all prohibited from baking flour belonging either to burgesses or country people, under threat of a large fine, £40 Scots.[24] This later entry appears very oddly among sixteenth century business, a clear case of a mistake by the binder.

The order made by deacon and council on 23 January 1643 that members of the Trade must not provide buns, fine bread, cakes and baps for taverns and brewers is more understandable; the innkeepers were making extra profit by reselling these items at marriages and feasts, profit the bakers felt should be their own.[25] This last order appeared among other regulations, however, which all seem to be aimed at controlling output and profits. For instance, some bakers were producing more bread than the deacon and council felt necessary and were also making unleavened white bread. The Trade ordered that only 60 stones of flour should be baked at one time, only £8 worth in the oven at one time and absolutely no unleavened bread. Bakehouses were often shared by several bakers and such statutes and ordinances would help to ensure fair, amicable and efficient use of the ovens.

Another complaint dealt with at the time was that bread was being sold outside the burgh at a higher price so that within Dundee prices could be cut. The Trade decreed that in future only 4s. profit in 20s. should be taken in the countryside, instead of the 7s. or 8s. objected to, and in the burgh there was to be no undercutting below the price of baking unless some large spender was buying 10s. worth or more. All of these practices were to be heavily fined in the future.

Unfortunately, with no other records to consult for the period it is impossible to tell if these rules were kept or produced income for the Craft as opposed to individual bakers. They were not recorded again in the Lockit Books, but neither were they repealed. In the next century what may have been another method of attracting custom was censured by the Trade's ruling body. Some craftsmen had been exceeding the traditional number of thirteen to the 'baker's dozen' and in future this was to be adhered to, unless other baxters or their wives were being served. The fine imposed on those who broke this rule started at £6 and then rose first to £10 and then to £20 Scots.[26]

In the last decade of the seventeenth century, when grain was in short supply, several ordinances were passed to try to prevent profiteering. When William Davidson was deacon in November 1698 it appeared that some bakers had been buying up all the wheat they could, both in and out of the burgh, and employing others to buy for them. The grain was then sold at high prices during dearth and, what was perhaps even more reprehensible to Dundonians at the time, sold to 'strangers', people from outside the burgh. It was pointed out that these practices threatened the liberties of the Trade as the supplies of other bakers were so curtailed that they were unable to 'serve the lieges'.

Such a situation gave the magistrates an opportunity to encroach on the trade's privileges. They might even go so far as to bring in unfree bakers, as the council's clear duty was to ensure a steady supply of food for the town. In light of the past relationship between council and Craft, such a prospect must have been very unwelcome. The Bakers decided to protect their position by fining offenders £5 Scots for every boll they sold outside the burgh or to anyone inside who intended to sell it beyond the burgh bounds.[27]

In 1699, when the export of any food from the town must have seemed extremely foolish to the residents, it is unsurprising to find that it was considered a 'great prejudice' to bake biscuits for skippers or seamen to use on their ships. But one wonders why bakers were told they must not sell buttered or unbuttered biscuits to any townsmen not in the Baxter Craft.[28]

A year later in 1700 and again in 1703 price cutting roused the Trade's collective wrath, as it had done 80 years before. Some members were selling bread cheap, typically the twelve penny loaf for ten pence, which the trade declared was at a loss and against the normal custom in most of Scotland. A £10 Scots fine was to be imposed but it would appear that some had found their way round this condition for in 1703 the additional rule had to be made that the price of bread sold in or for country markets should also be maintained at the regulation price.[29]

The Baker Craft may have been wealthy in 1486 but its economic life was a chequered one in the next hundred years. As we have seen, the bakers were not too happy with the treatment meted out to them by the magistrates. At a large meeting on 19 October 1573 during the deaconry of one of the several David Tendalls who held the post, the poverty of so many of their brethren in the Trade was attributed to the 'persecution' of the bailies. Insistence on specific weights for bread without regard to the various costs incurred such as the market price of the raw materials, transport and the varying charges for fuel, was what particularly upset the Craft.

They decided to augment their existing poor fund derived from the usual sources – fines for misdemeanours, etc. The deacon and 56 masters instituted what was to be known as the St Cuthbert's pennies. Bakers had to contribute to this each week whether they baked or not, 3d. for each baking, 1d. weekly from non bakers and from servants in the bakehouses and three half pennies for each batch. All had to be collected by a freemaster each Sunday who would be fined 2s. if he was slow – 'slothful' – in delivering the weekly pennies to the deacon.[30] During the following centuries steps were regularly taken to increase such payments as need arose.

All Trades tried to give some help to their needy brethren and their dependants but rarely does one find poverty attributed so specifically to one cause. As the Baxters felt driven to such drastic steps by the magistrates' threats to their privileges, they decided that it would be in order for the council of the Craft to borrow from this fund 'for the relief and defence of their liberties' if these seemed threatened in the future. This clause enabled later bakers to use their poor box money for court cases without any doubts about the legality of such a step.

Another sign of pressure on the Trade is that they showed nervousness about their numbers and about the quality of their entrants towards the end of the sixteenth century. In October 1578 at a meeting in the Howff, the Craft had made a unanimous decision that apprentices should pay a flat rate of £10 with no other exactions when their names were entered in the Lockit Book. It was particularly noted that they were excused from the former practice of giving a dinner to the rest of the Trade. Similarly, on becoming master and setting up his work stall, the newly qualified craftsman was asked to pay the same amount with no 'bankett'. These reduced entry fees must have been a considerable relief to those men at the beginning of their careers and probably encouraged a greater number to consider entering the baking trade.[31] Ten years later a different song was being sung.

There were poor harvests in the last decade of the sixteenth century but before the bakers could have been seriously affected, there were signs of disquiet, first appearing in concern about their increasing numbers. The first Lockit Book shows a marked disproportion of apprentices being entered compared to masters, almost 70 between 1558 and 1584 compared to under 20 masters. Lists of masters are recorded but few individual dates of entry, while over 60 are attested by a public notary in 1583.[32] (The query must arise – were masters entered in another place, despite the appearance of the usual type of ordinances, etc., in this volume?) On 5 February 1588 a twenty-one year ban was imposed on taking on any new apprentices after the tenth day of that month.[33] This was signed by 28 masters, a notary public acting for others. There was an immediate rush in the next few days when five were indentured and then a further seven, followed by a gap.

Despite the moratorium, the bakers were still complaining five years later that they and their predecessors had been 'greatly damnified' and driven to extreme poverty because of the excessive number of apprentices enrolled. They claimed that as a result many bakers had had to seek other ways of earning their living so that they could pay their taxes.[34] A further restriction was imposed, this time for sixteen years, confirming the original twenty-one. Any who did join had to pay punitive fees of £40 and give a banquet for their fellows both on the occasion of their becoming apprentices and then at their entry as masters. Nine new masters were admitted in the next three years and in 1596 further concern is shown when it was decided that even freemasters' sons, who were always shown some leniency when they applied to join, should give proof of their ability by an essay performed before all the Craft. If they did not give satisfaction they were 'repudiated' for a year and a day when they could re-apply.[35]

The ban on taking apprentices was relaxed temporarily in December 1610 and several immediately seized the opportunity despite the imposition of extra demands on the boys, or perhaps one should say on their parents or sponsors – wine for the Trade, an extra year's service in the bakehouse.[36] Stricter rules regarding their behaviour appear in 1615; absenteeism, disobedience and what sounds like 'moonlighting' – baking bread outside the burgh without the deacon's permission – being particularly frowned on.[37] Three years later, the earlier prohibition was repeated and laxity regarding burgess status was also to be fined.[38] On 7 June 1619 the bakers' court even stipulated the amount of food that could be provided during the mandatory year in the bakehouse – an eightpenny loaf from each baking.[39]

The reduction in the numbers of apprentices did not seem to affect the intake of masters for there are regular entries throughout these years, while concern is still voiced about the increasing number of the poor of the Craft. The entry fee became 40 merks plus a dinner.[40] There had been an earlier sign of financial problems in March 1614. Then the dues paid by each master both for baking and not baking were increased substantially. The payment of 6d. Scots for each baking and 1d. from each master who was not baking, 6d. for each 'baking of bakes' and 1d. for each servant became 12d., 2d., 8d. and 2d. Mention was made of both oat and wheat. Presumably 'bakes' were some special type of bread or roll.

Though most masters were probably working bakers, three men were entered in the Lockit Book in 1629 who can only have been there in an honorary capacity.[41] It is unlikely that David Graham of Fintrie, Mr John Fotheringham, brother german to the laird of Powrie, both members of the local county gentry, and Mr John Russell, an Edinburgh advocate, meant to 'serve the lieges' in Dundee by baking bread. In 1660 the contemporary laird of Powrie, another David, also took the oath of fidelity to the Trade.[42] It is possible that the estates of these men provided the bakers with meal. The connections were certainly kept up in the next century when Robert Graham of Fintrie became a master, as did David Wedderburn of the Ilk in September 1730,[43] and the Earl of Strathmore and James Fotheringham, merchant son of Thomas of Powrie in 1740.[44]

On two occasions, with 251 years between them, concessions were made to allow easier access to the privileges of the Trade when some extra service had been given. In 1557, James Duncan, oldest son and heir of a free master, was made a full master despite not having completed his indentures, because 'of the good deeds done by James at their command'.[45] What these good deeds were we are left to guess. In 1808, a journeyman, John Boyle, was admitted to being a free apprentice with the possibility of becoming master for only £10 whatever the normal fee might be at his entry. He had discovered a method of supplying barm – yeast – cheaply.[46]

As far as ordinary members were concerned, enrolment was healthy throughout the history of the Baker Trade. The Trade was powerful enough in its own field to insist on masters' performing essays as long as its privileges existed legally. As late as April 1846 an unfree applicant had to perform an essay before he was entered. In September 1825 the essay piece had been dispensed with in the case of a confectioner, but the entry included the note that this was 'in no way to be constructed a precedent'. There had been several entries of 'confectioners', the first James Keilor (*sic*) on 29 January 1805, but the only information about his entry was that he had paid £30, the sum 'agreed to be accepted' by the Trade. Other confectioners joined in the next decade but apart from honorary members few new masters specified any other qualification, so presumably they were bakers.

In the late eighteenth century there were over a dozen entered as coming from London, who seemed to be accepted without difficulty, some of them having Dundee connections. One was not so fortunate. In the 1760s Thomas Thain, who may have been a trail blazer for outsiders, was asked to perform what he considered an unreasonable test of his qualifications and in 1769 he was refused permission to carry out his trade in the burgh.[47]

The loss of burghal and craft privileges in 1846 seems to have had little impact in the long run on enrolment in the Trade. There were no new members from 1846 until 1854 but in that year, after a special resolution by a General Meeting of the Trade, James Gordon, a corn merchant, was entered as unfree, paying £7.10s. on 14 November.[48] James Petrie became deacon that year and he may have been responsible for a drive for members during his term of office. In September 1856 four bakers and one merchant joined, all unfree, and two months later twelve new masters included six corn merchants, one miller, three bakers, one merchant and one shipowner. It can be argued that the work of most of these has a connection with the baking trade, though it must be tenuous where the last two are concerned.

Since then, the Trade has recruited new masters fairly steadily and has maintained its basic foundations without becoming exclusively a bakers' club. The famous Dundee city engineer, James Thomson, joined in 1910; in 1937 a lithographer and a musical instrument dealer, Robert James Lang, were among the five entrants in the Lockit Book. It is a splendid continuation of an old tradition, however, that the names of today's well-known Dundee bakers are almost all recorded; many must have joined not long after setting up business in the town. Wallace is the oldest from centuries ago, and we have noted the appearance of Keillor, but Kidd, Nicoll and Smibert, Lightbody, Goodfellow all have joined the ancient brotherhood in the nineteenth and twentieth centuries as they set up their businesses in the town, having learned their trade elsewhere. Indeed bakers from other towns near Dundee – Perth, Aberfeldy, Methil, to mention only a few – are currently members.

Like the other Dundee trades, the Bakers showed their respect or gratitude to various eminent men by giving them honorary membership. On

10 October 1862, Sir John Ogilvy of Inverquharity, MP for Dundee burgh, and Sir David Baxter of Kilmaron joined the Trade. Winston Churchill too became a master in 1909 when he was one of the local MPs, though not all the members were pleased that they had to hold a joint meeting with the Bonnetmakers to admit him, as he had only half an hour to spare![49]

In the twentieth century bakers continue to maintain their interest in improving the craftsmanship of their trade. William Forwell left £300 in 1926 to promote the technical education of young bakers and each year an award is made to a deserving bakery student. One of the avowed aims of the Baker Trade, through the centuries, to serve the lieges, is still pursued by local members of the Craft. The continued existence of local bakers' businesses and Dundonians' support of these attest the success of their efforts in achieving this laudable ambition.

NOTES

[1] DDARC, GD/TD/B1.1.2 *passim*. The first Lockit Book of the Trade, 1554–1758, has been paginated and page numbers will be given in the notes. The second was in use from 1758–1988 and as it is the only source for much of the material in this chapter for events occurring during that period it will not be automatically cited.

[2] A. Maxwell, *Old Dundee, Ecclesiastical, Burghal and Social, prior to the Reformation* (Dundee, 1891), 30. Hereafter Maxwell, 1891. Unfortunately he did not give the document's whereabouts.

[3] DDARC, GD/TD/B1.1, p. 3.

[4] DDARC, GD/TD/B1.2; Baker Trade's Minute Book (hereafter BTMB) 1884–1988. This is in the custody of the Trade's clerk.

[5] DDARC, GD/TD/B1.2.

[6] E.P.D. Torrie, *Medieval Dundee*, Abertay Historical Society Publication No. 30 (Dundee, 1990), 66. Hereafter Torrie, 1990.

[7] A.H. Millar, *Glimpses of Old and New Dundee* (Dundee, 1925), 78–79. Hereafter Millar, 1925.

[8] DDARC, GD/TD/B1.1, p. 136, 4.3.1614.

[9] Ibid., p. 161.

[10] H.J. Dandie, *The Story of the 'Baxters'* (Aberdeen, 1990). My thanks to Mr David Goodfellow for the loan of this useful work. Hereafter Dandie, 1990.

[11] I.F. Grant, *The Social and Economic Development of Scotland before 1603* (1930), 399. Hereafter Grant, 1930.

[12] Maxwell, 1891, 227.

[13] Ibid., 344.

[14] Ibid., 226, 227.

[15] Ibid., 226, 227.

[16] Dandie, 1990, 59.

[17] DDARC, GD/TFD/B1.1, second entry.

[18] Ibid., p.144.

[19] GD/TD/B1.2, 23.11.1780.

[20] Ibid., 25.11.1795.

[21] 39 Geo. III c. 55.

[22] DDARC, GD/TD/B1.2, 22 November 1796.

[23] DDARC, GD/TD/B1.1, p. 237.

[24] All references, nos. 24–45 are from the first LB so only page numbers will be given. 42.

[25] 342.

[26] 343.

[27] 48, 21.11.1698.

[28] 48, 13.3.1698.

[29] 49, 50 – 5.11.1700, 9.1.1703.

[30] 55.

[31] 77.

[32] 85.

[33] 92.

[34] 102.

[35] 106.

[36] 122.

[37] 139.

[38] 147, 149.

[39] 152.

[40] 153.

[41] 183.

[42] 230.

[43] 286.

[44] 298.

[45] 7.

[46] DDARC, GD/TD/B1.2, 6.9.1808.

[47] Warden, 1872, 47.

[48] DDARC, GD/TD/B1.2. is the source for all LB references in the remainder of this chapter.

[49] BTMB, 12.10.1909.

CHAPTER 5

The Cordiner Trade – The Shoemakers

Cordiner is the old Scottish name for a shoemaker. Both terms were used throughout the ages but in the eighteenth century the entries to the Lockit Book gradually changed so that 'shoemaker' predominated. It is interesting, however, that when entering honorary members the old name was used for a much longer time.[1] Though the second trade in order of precedence, the earliest clue to the formation of the Dundee shoemakers into an incorporation seems to be a reference in 1522 to their letters of privilege.[2] If indeed they obtained a Seal of Cause before or about that time, this would be consistent with the history of the others who make up the Dundee Nine Trades. The Cordiner Trade owns two Lockit Books which throw little light on the subject, the older having entries of apprentices since 1560, and masters since 1590, but neither mentions or quotes a Seal of Cause.

However, an extract from Dundee town council records quoted by Warden indicates that the Trade was treated as if it did indeed have a charter endowing it with the usual privileges of incorporated crafts.[3] An act of the council of 20 May 1656 was the response to a supplication of the Cordiner Craft, handed in by the deacon of the time, Thomas Thomson. In this request the Cordiners asked for the ratification of the ancient liberties, rights and privileges formerly enjoyed by them. They requested too that encroachments on these rights should be forbidden in the future. The council not only agreed but added the qualification that none but members of the Cordiner Trade should even sell any type of footwear in Dundee apart from children's. The penalty was to be the confiscation of any such goods, half the value going to whoever reported such a breach of privilege, the other half to the council.

The older Lockit Book has been rebound since Warden examined it, for on the first page we now find 'Ane memorandun of the shoemakers of Dundee' concerning the repair of the 'sait' out of their chantry. This included a list of 58 names with the sums of money they were to give and also committed future masters to contribute as the Trade decreed.

Next follows an agreement made by the Nine Trades, then a list dated 10 September 1718 of those who had paid for their seat in the church and for the use of the mortcloth, with rules for future entrants. At last we come to the contents as Warden found them. Another oddity has arisen from the rebinding. In the middle of the book several older pages have been inserted concerning the purchase of two velvet mortcloths on 4 February 1634, one large and one small. Only the 35 masters who had contributed towards these cloths or those masters who paid their dues in the future were to be allowed to use them. The sum demanded was £3 Scots.

The older existing book may not have been the first the Trade used. Though the first master was entered in 1590, the several pages of ordinances and decrees are dated 13 January 1567 (i.e. 1568 as the year began in March at that time) slightly later than the first apprentice entry. Entries of masters in the next Lockit Book, still in use, began in 1774 but apprentices continued to be entered in the older volume until 1790. A new book opening in the later part of the sixteenth century would, like the probable date of the Seal of Cause, tie in with the history of the other Dundee Trades most of whom seem to have opened new books about that time. Both the apprentice list and the rules of the Trade must have been copied about 1589 or 1590, either from loose documents or from an even older volume.

Eight years after the current Lockit Book was opened in 1774 some members who had been entered before that time and the relatives of some deceased requested that the names from the old book should be recorded in the new one. They probably did not want to risk there being any doubt about their rights, and the demand shows some lack of faith in their administration. Whatever their reasons, their request was granted and on 7 October 1782 when Andrew Gray was deacon, the names of 53 earlier masters were listed, beginning with James Gray, 14 April 1696.

The history of the Cordiners is not dramatic. Like the other trades, they kept a close watch on the standard of work produced by their members. In their first statutes recorded, those of 1567, the deacon and other 'wysest men' on the Trade are authorised to inspect the new member's finished goods and remove such products if they considered the goods were not of a high enough standard. No time limit is set for this action, so masters were liable to have their work inspected throughout their working lives.

Another aspect of their concern for quality is their objection to the entry of sons or sons-in-law of masters who had not been fully trained in the craft. No other incorporation seems to have felt so strongly about this matter. From the end of the sixteenth century there are occasional attempts to eradicate a practice that the Trade felt might result in damage to their reputation. On 10 January 1597, it was decreed that masters' sons should perform the same sort of essay as other entrants, though paying only 40s. Scots as opposed to six merks plus a dinner to the Trade paid by unfree entrants. The first masters entered in the earlier Lockit Book had had to produce for their essay or masterpiece shoes, single and double boots and mules, both single and 'battered'. (Battered must mean that some sort of glue was used in their construction but what 'single and double' footwear can be is difficult to imagine.)

That act was not wholly effective. Nor does the Trade seem to have kept the ordinance of 5 October 1614, made at a meeting in the Cross Kirk which annulled an earlier act that allowed them to grant craft privileges to the husbands of masters' daughters. They bewailed the bad effects this act had provided. Over 100 years later, meeting at the Howff on 4 March 1730, they were once again expressing concern about the admittance of masters' sons who were not properly skilled in their trade. It was claimed that the main reason for the bad reputation of the Trade's products at the time was the inefficiency and lack of interest in improving their skills demonstrated by both masters' sons and sons-in-law who were allowed to enter the Trade after a 'superficial essay' was performed.

The town was said to suffer as well as the Trade for the inhabitants of Dundee were being forced to go elsewhere for fashionable shoes. This was the accusation against the Trade made by the town council, (as we have seen in Chapter Three,) and the insistence on more rigid testing was probably the Trade's defensive reaction. To ensure better workmanship a fairly hefty essay was set for both these categories of entrants. A pair each of Jaikt or strong boots, light boots, sea boots, men's shoes with timber heels, another pair with leather heels, men's pumps, women's shoes 'according to the fashion of the time' and a pair of spatterdashes or buttoned boots must have taken some time to make. John Nicoll, a freeman's son-in-law was entered a few years later with the pointed comment that he had made a sufficient say.[4]

All the work specified in 1730 had to be prepared in the would-be master's own house, under the eye of two specially appointed masters.[5] However, the Trade did not insist at this time on the conditions imposed on 31 December 1591 to prevent the offer of 'colorit seys', false work not in fact done by the applicant. At that date, the craftsman had to perform his essay after being locked in a 'close house' by the deacon and brethren, the deacon keeping the key until the work was completely finished. Thereby it was ensured that the essay offered was in fact the man's own work. Such a rule is not commonly found in the existing Dundee Trades' acts and ordinances.

In 1591 the Trade also decided to admit no stranger into their brotherhood unless he had served an apprenticeship in the burgh. The only exception was to be a master's son-in-law. In the earlier days of the incorporation members had to practise only in the burgh of Dundee or risk losing their privileges.[6] The poor lists of other trades show that they certainly did not adhere to such a law for recipients came from all the airts. As we have no Cordiners' lists it is impossible to check if they kept that rule for long, or at all, and the available records shed no light on this question.

Like all the Dundee Trades the Cordiners sometimes allowed a man to enter for his own life only. A life member paid only for himself, and his posterity had no claim on trade funds. Some entered on the condition that they could alter their status and many did, for it was a better bargain for one's posterity. Sons could then enter the Trade cheaply as masters' sons and all could claim from the poor box. The Cordiners, for some reason, were more inclined to accept members for their own life only than other Trades.[7] One eminent Cordiner, Archibald Walker, changed on 16 October 1750 to being a full member when he was deacon-convener of the Nine Trades, having joined as a life member in 1716. Warden claims from his inspection of the Cash Book, part of the Trade's archive which is now missing, that his change of status was given him free by the Trade.[8]

One important aspect of training in a craft was of course the years spent as a journeyman or servant of a master. Some masters were tempted to give work to journeymen to handle on their own. This practice always met with the Trade's disapproval as it allowed servants to encroach on trade privileges, claiming that their work was actually a master's. At the Howff on 8 October 1722, it was decreed that in future journeymen should be employed only in freemasters' houses and were not to be furnished with material for boots, shoes, slippers or clogs. The penalty for breaching this rule was seizure of the goods which would be sold for the poor, plus a fine first of £6, then of £12. In 1730 the Cordiner Trade insisted on a four-year period at the end of the apprenticeship to hone a man's skills, much longer than was the norm, before he could try for his entry as freemaster. This requirement must have tempted many to break the rules.

Apprentices were strictly disciplined everywhere and almost all indentures laid down that the boys should be loyal to their masters and generally honest. The shoemakers went further. Any apprentice found stealing was to be given forty strokes with a whip on his first offence. Continuing such wicked behaviour could result in his possessions and his cautioners' being confiscated and his expulsion from the Trade.[9] The 1567 rules were still adhered to almost 200 years later. In 1737 George Donet was subjected to a whipping and expulsion.

Warden quotes from records, which are now missing, recording the employment of journeymen, which all the incorporations maintained in theory but which are in fact rarely comprehensive. In short extracts he gives examples of three who left their masters illegally, but gives no indication of the proportion in this category. He declares that journeymen left their post 'frequently' but no conclusions can be drawn from the limited information he provided.[10]

One very interesting feature found by Warden in records of the Cordiners, also now missing, is the journeymen's 'Club' of the eighteenth century. (This is discussed in Chapter One.) One indication that it may have been a recognised part of the Trade can be found in an entry in the Lockit Book in 1723. It was then decreed that no journeyman should be employed by masters or masters' widows without informing the deacon, no matter whether the employee was 'stranger, club, or other'. There are other signs that the organisation, whatever it was, existed under the aegis of the Trade. On 5 November 1755 John Airth promised to pay the Shoemaker Trade £2 Scots 'as usual' and when John Kidd became journeyman to William Maiden he entered 'by way of Clubb' in 1726.[11] Lacking the actual documents we can unfortunately now only speculate about the nature of this club, but it is certainly unusual.

One arrangement made by the Cordiner Trade with their fellow Trade in Brechin may be unique among the Dundee Trades but with so many records missing, it is dangerous to be dogmatic about such things. In October 1600 the two incorporations in the persons of their deacons, Thomas Low in Brechin and John Rankin in Dundee, agreed that each could trade in the other's markets on equal terms. Goods were not to be inspected and no duties were to be paid. The agreement ends with the statement that the Brechin men were to frequent the Dundee market and the Dundonians that in Brechin as freely as they had in the past.

Unfortunately, there is no indication as to why the two incorporations felt they had to formalise at that particular time what had apparently been an accepted practice. The Trade seems to have had amicable relations with those of other burghs besides Brechin for the cash book seen by Warden recorded donations to other Trades – £6 to the Arbroath Trade in 1740 and £3 to shoemakers in St Andrews in 1743.[12]

The Cordiners were also distinctive among the Dundee Nine Trades in that there was no altar in the town kirk to the patron saint of shoemakers, St Crispin. It would have been unusual for their Seal of Cause to lack the undertaking to support an altar. The Cordiners compromised by contributing to the Halie Bluid altar and they processed there each Thursday after Trinity Sunday, keeping this as St Crispin's Day.[13] After the Reformation such ceremonies gradually died out in face of the disapproval of the new kirk but the St Crispin tradition survived until the eighteenth century. Somehow the saint was transformed into a king or champion.

The Cordiners' room in the Trades Hall was decorated with a frieze on the wall just below the cornice which illustrated such a procession with a Dundee background. It was commissioned from Alexander Methven, a housepainter and an amateur artist, but unfinished until 1822 when another young Dundee artist, Henry Harwood, completed it in time for George IV's visit. This was the last occasion when the Crispin procession took place. The frieze can now be seen in Dundee's McManus Galleries, having been saved before the hall was demolished.[14]

One of the Trade's privileges was their power to inspect hides at the market. (Once again we are dependent on Warden for information.) This may have been parallel to or have arisen about 1650 from a resolution made by the deacons of the 'Incorporated Trades'.[15] As a result of protestations made by the Cordiners the deacon of the Cordiner Trade with his council was authorised to go through the burgh and carry out a search wherever they suspected there might be badly tanned leather or other poor quality stuff used in making shoes. Any unsatisfactory material was to be confiscated.

The search of the market too could ensure that hides were correctly treated, that any customs due were being paid and that no-one was selling or buying unless privileged to do so in Dundee. Fines would be imposed on those found breaking the rules. Warden suggests that they farmed out this power, sometimes to one of their members. It would then be up to the farmer of the customs to make what he could from fines while the Trade was sure of a fixed amount of money. This was a common procedure in dealing with taxes in Scotland. The practice of examining hides lasted until 1784 by which time the income provided was very small, decreasing from 19s. in 1771 to an unspecified amount.[16]

Like all the incorporations, the Cordiners had their ups and downs. The first half of the eighteenth century was one period when the town as a whole was not in good heart. The Cordiners' records give some inkling of how they were affected. The attempt to control and restrict entries of masters' sons and sons-in-law by insisting on very testing essays was one example. In 1723 their debts were causing alarm and the solution was to ask each master to pay 6d. Scots weekly for both himself and each journeyman he employed, with the threat of loss of privilege for any who were 'obstreprous' about paying these contributions.[17] They kept their funds in two boxes, the principal box and the little box, unlike most of their fellow craftsmen.[18]

The numbers joining the Trade have gradually declined throughout their history. Warden attributes the decrease in numbers in the second half of the seventeenth century to the effects of Monck's sacking of the burgh, but there were other reasons for the state of Dundee's economy then.[19] The only fillip to numbers was in the third quarter of the eighteenth century when all the incorporated trades did well.

Thereafter industrial changes made for a different situation. Even before the loss of craft privileges, there had been a decline in entries of masters, with no new members joining between 1832 and 1844. Three more names appear between then and September 1859, and in the next two years, seven men joined the Trade. David Archer was the first of these and his sons entered immediately after him but this momentary enthusiasm did not last. Apart from the entry of two honorary members, Sir John Ogilvie and David Baxter, in 1862, there were no more until 1875. Twelve more were added to the ranks by 1912 by which time 129 masters had joined since 1774.

Until 1935, when the only extant minute book begins, there were no further entries. In that year the Trade took a new lease of life with the recruitment of butcher, William Clark, and a solicitor, Edward Simpson, both members of various other Trades as well. Alexander McGowan who had joined in 1896 became deacon. Since then just over 40 men have joined. The names of mid-twentieth century entrants include those of the owners of shoe shops, a few of which survived for some decades the overwhelming onslaught of the chainstore; others are leather merchants. Since 1947 the professions of the new cordiners has not been mentioned, but the Trade does try to maintain a connection at least with the old craft among members.[20]

Though the Trade's list of records and artefacts ordered in 1597 was never made, they have been quite fortunate since their revivification in the 1930s. The story of the recovery of their old Lockit Book, has already been told.[21] Two years before it was found, in 1938, a Miss Smith, identified only as 'of Tayport', gave Mr Clark two old silk flags and a flagpole top piece to hand over to the deacon. A Joshua Smith entered the Trade in 1861 and was followed by his son-in-law and son in 1885 and 1900. The likelihood is that Miss Smith was one of his descendants. Both flags had the shoemakers' crest, and one, dated 1863, was assumed to be a replacement for an older one.

The Trade also received the receipt for a lair in the Eastern Cemetery in the name of the deacon. In 1949 a former deacon, James Dunbar Hardie, who was entered as master in 1938, presented a chain of office for the use of the deacon. It was first worn at the Kirking of the Trades in October 1950. In September 1961 another former deacon, Mr R. Ogilvy Smith, made it possible for the Trade to provide retiring deacons with a badge.[22]

Another gift was a collection of foreign footwear belonging to Deacon Cuthbert. He was to show these for a time in his shop and then the City Librarian was offered custody of these interesting articles. Unfortunately, the sederunt book does not record what eventually happened to these 42 pairs of shoes.[23]

The documents handed over by Mr Mann in 1940 included some sasines of property. Like all the Trades, the Cordiners sometimes invested their funds in buying houses to let. One in which they had an interest was the Wooden Land, a timber fronted building on the north side of the Overgate, one of the oldest buildings in the burgh when it was demolished in 1876. According to A.H. Millar, one room within was furnished with shoemakers' benches which were let on a weekly rent.[24]

Not until 1757 is there any overt mention in the earlier Lockit Book of members having to swear any oath. Such an omission does not indicate that this did not occur, of course. The Cordiners would expect new members to swear allegiance to the Trade when they joined and the practice continues to the present day. Just after the Trade renewed its active life in the 1930s an unnamed member commented on the unsuitability of the wording of the oath.[25]

This was not the first time there had been an objection from a shoemaker to the undertaking he had to give on his entrance to the Trade. In 1792 there was still active interest in political reform in Dundee and Andrew Brown refused to adhere to the first clause by which he would submit himself to king and government in everything lawful with regard to church and state. He was admitted but without any other records we cannot know if there were any objections to his stance from other members.[26]

The oath was not changed at that time to accommodate the doubts of any future radicals but as it contained the promise not to sell any 'strangers goods in name of my own', nor to deal with unfreemen, it was hardly appropriate for either manufacturers or retailers in the twentieth century. The changed wording was engrossed on the page of the current Lockit Book on 9 September 1937 just after the older form. It simply commits members to being peaceable members of society and of the Craft, to promoting its interest and that of widows and orphans. The only archaic wording remaining in the new oath is the promise to endeavour to promote 'concord where discord is', a desirable aim whatever the form of wording.

NOTES

[1] CLB2. Both this and the earlier LB, 1567–1774 are in the custody of the clerk of the Trade.

[2] Maxwell, 1891, 337.

[3] Warden, 1872, 385, 386.

[4] CLB1.

[5] Ibid.

[6] Ibid.

[7] Warden, 1872, 405.

[8] Ibid., 391.

[9] CLB1, 1567 statutes.

[10] Warden, 1872, 390.

[11] Ibid., 383, 389.

[12] Ibid., 404.

[13] Millar, 1925, 134, 135.

[14] Information beside the mural, now in Dundee McManus Galleries.

[15] Warden, 1872, 399.

[16] Ibid., 404–405.

[17] Ibid., 383.

[18] Ibid., 393, 394.

[19] Whatley, 1993, 62.

[20] Information from the clerk of the Cordiner Trade.

[21] See Chapter One, The Trades' Records, pp. 11–12.

[22] CSB, September 1961.

[23] Ibid., 24.10.1947; 17.9.1948.

[24] Millar, 1925, 134.

[25] CSB, 3.9.1936.

[26] CLB2.

CHAPTER 6

The Glover or Skinner Trade

The Lockit Book which Mr Lindsay deposited in Dundee Public Library in 1990 contains records of the Glover Trade dating from the middle of the sixteenth century. The Lockit Book currently in use was opened in 1607 and it was previously believed that no earlier records had survived. In the older book deacons' accounts, entries of masters and servants, statutes of the Trade all make their appearance; journeymen were entered in it until 1797. The last date for a master's entry was 1613 and it is likely that the clerk erred in not using the newer book in which masters were by then being entered. A decision made at a meeting of the Nine Trades was also recorded and this has been discussed in Chapter Three.[1]

In the old volume, no doubt because of the usual chaos that followed rebinding, entries are found made at random. Neither chronology nor subject help one to find one's way through the book. On the front fly-leaf it is recorded in an eighteenth century hand that the book was made for the use of the Glover Trade of Dundee in 1554. However, the earliest entry seems to be an apprentice's entry in 1560 and 125 boys' names are entered in the first pages before 1607, when the 'new' book, still in use today, was opened.

It is regrettable that one seventeenth century custom recorded in this volume was not maintained. When the deacon ended his spell of office, he handed over everything in his possession belonging to the Trade to be listed in the Trade's Book. In 1623 the list included the 'haill ornaments' of the Skinner Craft in a common kist as well as the Lockit Books and the 'Prising box' where the fees paid for valuing skins were kept; in 1627 a mortcloth, in 1628 in a new coffer; in 1630 a 100 merk bond and an ensign.

In 1673 though the 'ornaments' had vanished, more significant documents were mentioned. These were an act of council in favour of the Trade, presumably the Seal of Cause, and nine pieces of parchment concerning the Craft's rights. In 1676 these documents were once again noted when the deacon's accounts were approved but after that date if they were handed over they were not detailed in the Lockit Book. We can only be thankful that though the Skinners' Seal of Cause has long been lost, some provident masters decided to have it copied into the book opened in 1607.

The first entry in the current book is the oath sworn by entrant apprentices and new masters. The first clause of the oath makes the usual promises of obedience to God and attendance at church and reverence towards those who minister the blessed sacraments. The oath ends with what reads with unusual cynicism for the time. The new glovers are told they must maintain the religion 'presentlie expressit'. The remaining clauses followed the normal pattern – loyalty to the king, the provost and bailies and the laws they made for the good of the burgh, and obedience to the deacon of the Trade.

Some moral precepts follow on the next pages. Those who fear God and walk in his way are told they are blessed for 'of his Labor he sall eit'. They close with a little moral poem:–

> How happie ane thing it is
> and Joyfull for to sie
> Brethren Todigger fast to hald
> the band of amitie.

On page four of the current Lockit Book we find the 'Copie of ane of our letter inclosit in our common Kist'. This had been signed by the provost and bailies of Dundee on 12 January 1516 (1517 by today's reckoning) and confirmed by the king 'and his maist Noble Progenitors' in favour of the Skinner Craft of Dundee when James Makesoun was deacon.

The Seal of Cause also followed the usual pattern. First the Skinners agreed to raise money 'yearly and perpetually' to look after the altar in the parish church in honour of Saint Dutho (sic) and Saint Martin, their patron saint, with a chaplain to 'sing and say' divine service daily before the altar. The precise location of the altar in the kirk was not specified as it is in some other cases.

Then followed the endorsement of existing rules already made by the Trade. Like the other Dundee Trades the Dundee skinners had certainly formed their own society, if not one officially recognised by the local authority, before the date of the Seal of Cause. These rules referred both to the general philosophy of craft behaviour and to specific needs of the Skinner Trade and were very similar to those in other Seals of Cause. The older Lockit Book refers to one statute made in 1517 which threatens expulsion from the Trade if any servant goes to market with any goods except his master's.

Anyone practising any part of the trade, from buying skins to working them, except under a free master had to pay 40 shillings Scots towards the upkeep of the altar, though freemen's sons were let off with 6s.8d. Master skinners had to become freemen of the burgh and give proof of their competence to the deacon and established masters, six of them at this time. A would-be master must also have served the appropriate number of years of apprenticeship laid down at any specific time. It was stated that 'Vagabonds and other loose men' were coming to Dundee from other places who had 'unperfytlie learnit' the craft.

The new Lockit Book was brought into use with all due ceremony. Craft and Town Council met in the Cross Kirk on 16 February 1607. Considering all this ceremony it is odd to find some discrepancy between the dates given in the older book as to the opening of the new. The new book is mentioned in it for the first time in 1620 but records began at once in the new volume.

At the official opening all the previous acts and statutes of the Skinner Trade were read and confirmed and set down in the new book as well as additional rules. These included the usual regulations regarding personal behaviour and respect for the Trade and its officials. Four masters, not six as in the earlier acts, had to examine the would-be entrant's essay which consisted of preparing a dozen watered and tanned leathers and a pair of double gloves, a pair of single gloves, a shooting glove, with a purse of 'haill' leather, a 'calit' bag (a satchel) and a dozen sufficiently hardened points (leather used as ties). None of the Trade's secrets were to be revealed. Apprentices had to serve six years plus one as a servant while it was decreed that a master could not take on an apprentice unless he had a wife and a house as well as enough resources to feed and train the boy.

Skins had to be tanned only in free masters' houses; the burn that ran in the Cowgate and the Wellgate was forbidden territory for soaking them. Skinners were not to work in taverns or brewhouses or they would be fined 40s. Tanned leather was not to be sold as 'wyle' – wild, i.e. unprepared; sheepskin was not to be used for a variety of goods such as ties for bags; and no badly tanned leather was to be used. Every Saturday or every fourteen days, and especially at the fairs, the deacon with some advisers was to examine all skinner work within the town and any made outside the town but brought in for sale by merchants and chapmen.

Some of these statutes are also to be found in the older book, such as the rule that a master must be married and fairly well-endowed before he could take an apprentice. A later statute, however, did not seem to need to be repeated in the new book. On 20 November 1653 the Trade ruled that 'neither masters, not widows nor none belonging to' the Skinner Trade should in future weigh goods for sale to any bonnetmaker or any other tradesman at more than 19 pounds to the stone. A large 20 merk fine was to be imposed. This rule demonstrates the volatility of Scottish weights as a stone was generally reckoned as 14lbs. It also seems to show that the Court of Session decree resulting from the Bonnetmakers' complaint made against the Skinners in 1611 had not been particularly effective. Then they had been ordered to sell their wool according to the weights of the weigh-house of Dundee.[2]

The new Lockit Book had been in use for some years when in 1616, a list of masters was copied 'out of an old book' belonging to the Craft which presumably was the volume now in Dundee's Central Library. The earliest master recorded was Thomas Innes who was booked on 8 May 1566 and a steady though small stream of skinners joined the craft until 1607 when there were 72 names in the book. As the Seal of Cause was dated 1516 there must have been earlier masters, perhaps an even earlier Lockit Book than that so recently rediscovered. James Stewart was the first master entered in the current book on 23 February 1608 and the total entered from 1566 to 1613 was 89.

Both Lockit Books are unfortunately all too reticent about many features of the Trade's history. For instance there are no comments on the reason for the Trade's beginning to call itself alternately Skinner or Glover from the 1660s. There is equal silence on the great 1819 controversy,[3] in which the Glovers were prominent with the other two small Trades. This action may have been discussed in any sederunt book the Trade possessed but if these do exist, they have not been available for research at this time and from the quotations A.J. Warden uses in *The Burgh Laws*, he saw only the newer Lockit Book, not even the rediscovered volume.

There was never a large number of Glovers, and recruits to the ranks of the incorporation decreased through the years. The whole of the eighteenth century saw just over 40 new masters and that total included honorary members such as George Dempster of Dunnichen, the Duke of Atholl and Admiral Lord Duncan of Camperdown. In the first half of the nineteenth century only four masters joined, two in 1824 and two brothers, James and Peter Stewart, in 1831. James called himself a glover, Peter a skinner. Their father, Thomas, had become a freemaster in 1798, and their paternal grandfather had hailed from Coupar Angus. There were no further entries until 1869 when on 28 December three of James Stewart's sons, James Arnott, David and Charles, joined the incorporation. David was a solicitor and the other two were merchants.

For the next half century, the Stewart family provided the main strength of the Trade. Peter had a daughter Jessie, whose husband was a corn merchant, but as a freemaster's son-in-law he was accepted as a master glover in 1885. The next entry on 11 October 1900 was that of William Ferguson Stewart a contractor in Queensland, Australia, whose brother Charles signed for him as his attorney. A bank clerk from East Newport whose middle name was Stewart joined the same day; he might have been one of the clan. Five days later, William Cummings Ferguson Stewart, son of the Australian contractor, himself a manufacturer, was also entered. When the next entrant, Thomas Stewart, a joiner, was booked on 3 November 1914, W.C.F. Stewart was deacon.

Recruitment to the Trade resumed in 1918 but Stewarts no longer figure in the short list of members entered up to 1980. Six Smiths and five Adams, four Laings and Wilsons, one Bruce, one Graham, one Lawson and one Campbell, minister of the Trades' kirk, make up the roll, and only two, Ralph Robertson Adams and Gavin George Adams, booked in 1955, gave their occupation as glovers. The majority of the others were manufacturers, one of silk, or clothiers, and were also unfree. More recruits to the Trade are essential to keep it in a healthy condition.

The incorporation like all the others did not always achieve all its aims. Masters sometimes had difficulty in keeping up their standards and in hard times could not always give as much succour to the poor of their Trade as they would have liked. The first complaint of hard times recorded in the Lockit Book came in 1659 when according to the deacon and the rest of the brethren, more funds were needed than the present entry fees and any capital they owned could provide. To ensure that 'decayed members' could be helped and the trade as a whole given encouragement, a charge of one penny Scots was imposed on each 'almet' skin, one that had been tanned by being soaked in alum. Any skinner who refused to pay could be charged 4d. by the deacon.

The same entry expressed alarm at the incompetence or neglect of those who had to apprize skins, evaluating them for sale and ensuring that they were of good quality and properly tanned. Responsibility was placed squarely on the deacon's head to remedy this. He had to make sure skins were properly apprized and then he had to collect them. Failure on his part was to result in his being fined double the duties.

The lack of records means that we cannot know whether this ever happened, but a few years later, on 10 October 1667, the craft decided to annul the act. Due to 'good administration and the blessing of God', they thought the extra charges were no longer needed. At the same time, however, there was concern at the poor work both made and brought into the burgh by the unfree. The deacon was asked to visit 'all such works' at his convenience and to censure 'insufficient' work according to the customs observed in other Royal Burghs.

This clause, added to that in the Seal of Cause on what those who were not working under a free master had to pay for skins, raises the question as to how much control the Trade ever exercised over non-members. It had always tried. The older Book records that in 1623, Mr James Wedderburn and seven of the Trade were authorised to search out insufficient work. However, if unfreemen could set up 'works' in the burgh and experience nothing but verbal criticism from the deacon, the Trade's authority in the burgh did not count for much. Their small numbers might have removed any fear of reprisals among interlopers while a complaint made in 1724 showed that even the magistrates provided themselves with wool and gloves from other places.

Glovers did not escape the common problems of the last decade of the seventeenth century, when all Scotland suffered economic troubles. On 15 October 1696, the Trade met and decided that the entry fee for a new master should be £40 Scots plus a 'sofichant' dinner for the Trade in an honest tavern. The only entry fee found in the Lockit Book before that date was noted in 1607 when it was 13s.4d. By 1696 it was probably more, but the new figure would be an increase to keep down entries as well as helping the distressed members of their society in these dreadful years.

Almost thirty years later, in 1724, there were more financial problems. The Glovers were again experiencing the same troubles as other craftsmen. The burgh's economy had not recovered from the disasters of the previous century. The Trades all believed that there were too many master crafts- men of all kinds, and the Glovers thought that half the actual numbers practising their trade would have been enough to supply Dundonians adequately. In an attempt to remedy this situation the entry fee for appren- tices was raised to £30 Scots and four years as a servant was demanded instead of the usual one or two. Further new masters were not to have a share in the skins bought at the market or anywhere else for two years after their admission.

These were fairly savage restrictions but two years later with the burgh's economy still in a deplorable state, too many master glovers were becoming bankrupt and calling on the Trade's poor fund. It was not possible even to purchase a new mortcloth though the existing one was in a 'low and mean state'. The solution was to impose £10 Scots on all future freemasters for maintenance of a new one and £1.10s. on freemasters' sons for the privilege of using it. Other methods of increasing their 'common stock' were to charge every stranger journeymen 1s. Scots for each week in service for three weeks. Then the master must book him in. It was on the same day, 1 December 1726, that a fee of £3 was also decided on for use of the house at the East Port where the Trade's skins were treated with lime.

Conditions were not much better a year and a half later. In April 1728, it was complained that despite an act of 1724 insisting on £30 Scots for every apprentice booked, they were still daily – perhaps an exaggeration considering the size of the incorporation – crowding into Dundee, becoming masters in due course. There were still too many to be able to provide for themselves and their families. Other Trades had raised their booking money for the same reason and the nine glovers present decided on £48 Scots as the entry fee to discourage prospective new apprentices.

Needless to say the cost of becoming a master glover did not remain static. Like all the other Trades at the time, the Glovers augmented the entry fees controlled by the Town Council by charging for 'accidents' like officer's fees. In 1750 John Walker married to Elizabeth Blair, a freeman's daughter, paid £60 Scots for booking money, £10 for the mortcloth, £3 for the East Port house and £8 officer's fee. Ten years later Daniel McIsack had to pay £100 Scots booking money plus £25 for the incidentals. Freemen's sons on the other hand were still paying only £1 sterling (£12 Scots) in the 1760s by which time the Trade was using both sterling and Scots.

There is one act of the Trade recorded in the Lockit Book, unfortunately undated. Just after an entry of 20 February 1634 reporting that Alexander Boyter had left the poor of the Skinner craft 100 merks, (£68.13s.4d. Scots) there is an undated entry. Written in a different hand and probably, from its position on the page, later than the notice of the legacy, it states that the craft has ordained that no-one should be admitted except freemen's sons or free apprentices. Similar attempts to prevent incomers to the burgh from joining are to be found in the records of other Trades, such as the Tailors. No repeal of this act has been found in the Lockit Book so presumably it fell into disuse when there was no longer need for it, or perhaps the Glovers simply forgot about it.

The few references in the Lockit Book to the finished products of the Trade give us no insight into the methods used in making them. Gloves, finished skins, bags, etc. may be mentioned as part of a master's testpiece, but only one sketch of a glove at the side of one entry in 1607 in the newer Book gives any indication of style and none of the methods used in making them. Their quality basically depended on the skins used being properly tanned but the only qualification made about the skins was that they must be 'sufficient'. The various processes are neither fully listed nor described.

Tanning or barking as it was called because tree bark was used in the process is a malodorous process which both town and craft tried to control. The magistrates as well as the individual deacons could examine skins and fine people like James Abernethy who had to pay 40s. for selling 'eveil barkit' leather.[4] We have seen that the Trade itself forbade soaking of leathers in the burn running between the Cowgate and the Wellgate, needed for domestic purposes. If the skinners were not careful they could contaminate the water needed for ordinary purposes by their neighbours. Sometimes they diverted streams and there was often trouble until they built their own 'work house'.

The Trade by 1750 owned the building, referred to as a house or work house, at the East Port where there were special pits for soaking skins. New masters had to pay towards the upkeep of the house and pits. John Walker as we have seen paid £3 Scots in 1750 among the other casualties when he was booked as master. Twenty years later, on 17 November 1770, the whole craft met and raised the dues because of the 'extraordinary expenses of the water pits'. All entrants to the Trade whether the sons of free or unfree were in future to pay £1 sterling as a down payment of double dues of 6d. per 100 skins each time they used the water pits.

By the last decade of the century, however, the numbers in the incorporation were very small and indeed, some might not have been glovers at all if they became masters as sons or sons-in-law of free masters. Perhaps as a result the limepits were unused and neglected. In 1794, it was decided to sell the house and ground. At the meeting held on 16 April it emerged that the house and dykes were 'entirely gone to ruin' and had not been used by any of the Trade for several years. The dunghill on the south end was excluded from the sale, as it was let to David Cobb with a tack that had still some years to run, but the sale raised £80. The following year £120 was deposited in the Dundee Bank, but there is no indication in the Lockit Book as to how the Trade had raised that amount.

A.J. Warden remarked at the end of his chapter on the Trade that it was believed to be wealthy.[5] If this belief was correct, it is a mystery as to where the wealth sprang from. The Lockit Book mentions only one legacy; the number of masters was always small and their entry fees were not exorbitant. The older Book certainly showed that they owned bonds to the value of 572 merks in 1662 but these disappeared from the records. Possibly the reticence on which Warden comments has led to his conception of the Trade's financial position. A page and a half of bonds dating between 1739 and 1768 appear in the later pages of the current Lockit Book showing what had been deposited with the society but most were shown as repaid. The only mention of money being deposited in a bank or anywhere else has already been mentioned. On the other hand when the sale of the work house was being discussed, the tack of the dung heap appeared almost incidentally. In light of the lack of any further archival material, there can be no certainty either way.

The entries in the Lockit Book show that the Glover Craft, never large, gradually shrank through the centuries to become a very small society indeed. A.H. Millar declared that there were ten members when he was writing.[6] Warden counted five and today's numbers cannot be very much more than a dozen unless there has been a great influx of members since the Lockit Book was studied for the purpose of this chapter.

NOTES

[1] Most of the material in this chapter is to be found in the Glover Trade's two Lockit Books, one in Dundee District Library, the current one in the custody of the Trade. It is usually obvious which is being quoted so no specific references to these works are given.

[2] BmT Archive. Bundle 8; See R.E. Zupko, 'The Weights and Measures of Scotland before the Union' in *S.H.R.*, lvi (1977), 137.

[3] See Chapter 3.

[4] Maxwell, 1891, 337.

[5] Warden, 1872, 420.

[6] Millar, 1925, 96.

4. ST ANDREW'S CHURCH

(Spanphoto, Dundee)

CHAPTER 7

The Tailor Trade

Fourth in precedence among the Nine, the Tailors have kept a careful watch over their records. Their archive contains many copies of official decisions at local and governmental level[1] and this makes it the more incomprehensible that their Seal of Cause is missing. Nor is it often referred to in their documents. The Nine Trades may have had it in their care or at least had a sight of it at one time, for there is one document listed in their inventory of writs,[2] 'The Seal of cause by the provost Baillys and town councill of Dundie in favor of the Deacon of the taylors and his succers (successors) In name of the sd taylor trade of the sd burgh Dated 8 December 1525'. This is the eighth document in the inventory and the ninth mentions yet another Seal of Cause in favour of the Tailor Trade dated 3 February 1594. Among those giving their consent to the later agreement is the minister, a possibility by that date.

Unfortunately, the date of entering these two documents in the inventory is not given. All that can be said is that the handwriting is of the eighteenth or early nineteenth century. It is also regrettable that only the titles of these documents have been entered in the inventory. The first six written in earlier handwriting were copied in their entirety but a later clerk has given merely extended titles to the remaining documents. The Trade itself had an inventory made at the end of 1842[3] when it was noted that they possessed 422 documents but that several regarding their privileges had been lost.

Presumably the Tailor Trade obtained their privileges with conditions attached similar to those in the Seals of Cause of the other incorporations. There is no evidence in their papers as to which altar they supported, if any. Warden names St Ann as the patron saint of tailors generally[4] but there are no other clues. The Lockit Book was opened in 1584 by which time the religious beliefs of the Reformers had banished from Scottish kirks all such symbols of 'idolatry' as altars for the worship of saints.

The Lockit Book itself is a small volume now kept in a velvet-lined box. A label inside indicates that it was on display at the 'Old Dundee' exhibition of 1892–93 held in the Albert Institute. It has been rebound at some time and the Trade's oath and the fees to be paid by new masters of all categories on their original paper have been inserted at the beginning. The first sum masters had to pay was at the 'First Court' – £3 Scots or 5s. sterling. Other Trades also used the term 'court' but no others seem to have made such a specific charge.

If A.J. Warden's description of the contents of the Lockit Book when he saw it[5] means that the first list of masters in 1567 appeared on the first pages, yet another binder unqualified as a palaeographer has been let loose on it since the 1870s. The 1567 entry is now preceded not only by the material listed above and an extract from the proceedings of the Convention of Royal Burghs of 10 July 1708 regarding the corruption in burgh councils but also by pages of later entries of masters and apprentices and deacons' intromissions. The dates of these entries swing from 1613–1627 then back to 1562, forward irregularly until 1687, when we at last find the 1567 opening.

From that time until today apprentices, masters and some statutes of the Trade have been entered with only a few aberrations in dates. For instance, between the entries of two free apprentices in October and November 1647, a decision of thirty masters of the Trade of 14 October 1618 is inserted, insisting that all masters should have served an apprenticeship to Dundee master tailors. It is upside down and the reason for this is not necessarily the binder's mistake but the result of a decision of the clerk of the time to begin a new category of record at the back or in the middle of the Book. This was a common practice. However, the Tailors seem to have recorded fewer of their statutes in their Lockit Book than most of their fellows did and many of their important decisions are to be found loose among their papers.

The Tailors also still have the book in which they recorded the names of many of the servants employed by free masters between 1637 and 1701.[6] In the decade before this book was closed a new type of servant appears – lads or boys. These may have been children who were not entering an apprenticeship or at least were not becoming free apprentices. The Trade might have attempted at least sporadically to maintain a record of all journeymen and obtain their booking fee, but in 1800 members who had defaulted were threatened with prosecution.[7] However a few months later they decided to stop taking money from journeymen.[8]

The conditions of employment laid down for the servants in the seventeenth century illustrate one of the means by which the Trade attempted to control their craft. The activities of journeymen as well as of unfreemen were restricted. When Andrew Palle entered James Merser's service on 6 June 1637 he promised, like many others recorded after him in the book, not to work as a tailor within four miles of Dundee. The draconian penalty of £100 was threatened. Others had the clause added 'except with a free master'. The second servant, whose name was entered in the book the week after Palle's, undertook not to live in the Hill but in the burgh of Dundee, while in September David Smyth undertook to pay his entry before he worked in the landward districts.

Different distances were decided on at different times and for different servants. In October 1638 three miles was the distance specified, four in December of that year, seven in 1652 and six on several occasions in 1653. In the 1660s and 1670s some servants were forbidden to 'shape, sew or take measure' of any Dundee inhabitants. Such a rule if adhered to would effectively have prevented their doing anything but repairs for the Dundee burgesses.

Tailors were one of the crafts most vulnerable to infringement of their privileges because of the nature of their work. Weavers were another. As well as having their own workshops they often worked in customers' homes, a practice that continued until modern times. The Dundee Trade petitioned the Convention of Royal Burghs in July 1587 for help in stamping out such opposition. Their complaint comprised all unfree workmen, saying that a great number of unfree – but especially of the Tailor Craft – 'were received, entertained and quietly maintained by freemen inhabitants of burghs within this realm within their private houses and dwelling houses'.[9] There would not even have been the sound of a sewing machine to betray a tailor who was employed illicitly.

The Convention responded by ordering the provosts and bailies of all burghs to attend to such infringements. At a meeting of the Dundee Head Court on 1 October 1587 no unfree workmen of any craft were to be allowed to work in the town and any inhabitants who employed them were to be fined 20s. each time they transgressed.[10] However, this law was to stand only as long as the inhabitants were properly served by the craftsmen and their servants.

The problem of weeding out unfree tailors had been recognised by the burgh authorities even before this date. In 1551 the bailies of Dundee allowed officers of the burgh with members of the Craft to visit private houses if such breaches of privilege were suspected.[11] In 1581 bailies instructed their officers to arrest offending tailors.[12] The lack of total success in even such draconian measures is to be found in their regular repetition with reinforcement of previous attempts.

In 1600 the Head Court commented that the acts and penalties were not regarded by the inhabitants, and increased the penalties to five marks towards the 'common works' of the town, (e.g. harbour repairs) from employers, and a 20s. fine on the workman; increased for further offences to 40s. and then to perpetual banishment. In addition any freeman employing such craftsmen was to pay the price of the labour of the work done to the poor of the Trade which had been damaged by such practices.[13] The same year saw the town council supporting statutes of the Trade which prohibited the employment of unfree tailors by the town's inhabitants, as long as there were enough freemen to serve the town and also as long as they kept their prices reasonable.[14]

Regardless of Trade, town council, Convention of Royal Burghs and similar laws passed by the Three Estates, Dundonians, both burgesses and indwellers, continued to employ these workmen who no doubt provided sufficient service at cheaper prices. In February 1620 the tailors complained once more about there being so many unfree workers that they were reduced to poverty and asked that houses should be searched more diligently.[15] Again in 1634 previous acts were ratified. If masters and magistrates were refused access to check on the employment of unfree workmen, then an oath was required from the citizen to the effect that he had never employed such labour. At the same time servants were permitted as in 1600 to mend clothes on their own.[16] In 1647 the ability to arrest offenders was confirmed[17] and in 1692 the Tailors had their privileges confirmed once more.[18]

The Trade tried to restrict the influx of outside workers to some extent by licensing some applicants and by prosecuting offenders. Burgesses who employed these workers as well as the workmen themselves were taken to court.[19] James Gib was very relieved not to be sent to prison in 1675 and he promised not to work in future 'to the prejudice of the Craft'.[20]

The Hill tailors posed particular difficulties for the Dundee Trade because of the nearness of Hill and burgh. It was too easy to transport cloth and clothes from one to the other. The Hill was also a magnet for unfree workers who knew they would find it an easy base from which they could slip into Dundee. Some Hill masters were among those obtaining licences to work in the burgh. In 1637 David Martine and his son William paid steeply – £100 Scots – so that they could 'measure and shape' within their own house but they were allowed to move themselves and their work between Hill and burgh without being troubled. They were restricted to only two servants, however, an apprentice counting as one of these.[21] Another Hill tailor had to promise not to work in the town while others paid for the privilege either in Dundee or the Hill.[22]

Difficulties between burgh and Hill continued even after Dundee absorbed the smaller settlement, and the Dundee Trade was also clearly

114

worried by those tailors who worked in the suburbs of Chapelshade and Blackscroft. In January 1765 a meeting of the Hill and Dundee masters agreed that there was need for proper organisation in these areas. It was agreed that a deacon or visitor and a boxmaster should be elected by the Trade's council and the Hill masters each year. Quarterly accounts were to be collected by these officers in the Hill and paid in at the Trade's Michaelmas entertainment while those tailors in the suburbs were to be prosecuted.[23]

There were still disagreements, however. In 1785, a Hill master, Patrick Thomson, was prosecuted at Forfar sheriff court for arrears of quarterly accounts. He retorted that certain bonds granted by him to the Trade absolved him from paying. The case might have reached the Court of Session; the Trade was adamant that it would go on as otherwise the Trade might lose its privileges in the Hilltown.[24] They employed an agent in Edinburgh and the case dragged on but by 1790 Provost Riddoch had been asked to use his good offices to try to settle the process.[25] Eventually Thomson settled for his costs, but the Trade had to borrow to pay him.[26]

The Thomson case might have been only the tip of an iceberg for in December 1790 the Hill masters wrote 'proposing to settle differences on matters of dispute between them and the Dundee Trade'. They offered £3.6s.8d. as entry fees to the Dundee Trade as well as money formerly paid to the Trade for freedom in the Hilltown and this offer was accepted.[27] Notwithstanding this agreement the Hill masters seemed to keep their distance, not often attending meetings of the Trade in the burgh. Tailors from the suburbs and the Hilltown continued paying the Trade to be allowed to sew in the nineteenth century.[28]

Many men also came into the burgh claiming the privilege of working as craftsmen without paying the local incorporations because they had served in HM Forces. Militiamen were in a grey area here[29] and eventually in 1819 the War Office wrote that service there only counted when a man had the freedom of the city in which he lived. The Shoemakers and the Tailors compared notes with Edinburgh and Glasgow incorporations[30] and took joint action against two men, one of whom decided he had no rights and the other paid the Shoemakers £5.[31] Even in 1846 the Trade pursued those they suspected of 'encroaching' and sold licences at 33s. to many.[32] They also passed a byelaw in 1829 forbidding 'packing and peeling' – any kind of dealings with unfree by members of the Trade – threatening fines and eventual loss of all benefits of membership.[33]

In the nineteenth century different types of competition appeared. London merchant tailors had taken to measuring for gentlemen's clothes and then sending the finished garments to their customers. In 1807 the Tailors sought legal advice as to whether such action was an encroachment on their privileges.[34] They stated that they had always considered taking measurements of the utmost importance and made it a particular part of the trial of masters on their admission. Their counsel, Mathew Ross, agreed where clothes made to measure were concerned and even seems to suggest that cash sent to pay for these garments could be arrested. He also thought that the tailors must show their Seal of Cause and if they had never had one, they should ask the magistrates for one. This suggestion does not seem to have been followed up.

In the 1820s the shape of stores to come reached the town. A Mr James Murison advertised a 'Wholesale and Retail Cloth Warehouse'. As well as offering clothes to be made by a first-class tailor, which cost 25 per cent less than Edinburgh and London charges and certainly less than any made to measure, this firm was stocking accessories – hats, gloves, stockings and ladies' riding habits. Another merchant, a Mr Gall sold haberdashery and meant to take custom to Dundee or Edinburgh tailors.[35]

Mr Murison asked the Trade in May 1829 if he could enter the incorporation. He meant to employ a journeyman. In 1767 the 'laudable custom' had been re-instated of making a new entrant measure the customer, cut the cloth, sew and finish off a garment in the presence of two masters who watched the whole process.[36] As it was believed that Mr Murison could not 'perform with his own hand the manipulations of the Trade', it was believed by members that some of the doubts about his being admitted were justified. After consulting the Perth and Aberdeen Trades it was decided that he would not be allowed to enter, though ex-deacon Beanston was in favour.[37]

To stop Murison's new venture in the burgh, and hopefully to prevent any others opening similar ventures, counsel was consulted – once again – and a long fight began against Murison. To start with it was argued that as Murison was a member of the Guildry and a draper, he could not exercise a craft if acts of the Scottish parliament 1466 c.12 and 1487.c.107 were still in force. Counsel agreed the Tailors were in the right but once again raised the vexed question of their Seal of Cause.

In 1833 Murison offered to pay £5 p.a. to the Trade, an offer which was scornfully refused. He agreed to produce an essay which the Trade would not pass, though the essay masters admitted it fitted. Not surprisingly his lawyer pointed out the difficulty of making it in the Tailors' Hall in the presence of people predetermined to find fault.[38] The Trade gave up the contest only when their appeal to the Inner House of the Court of Session against Lord Jeffrey's note on an interlocutor failed in December 1836.[39]

Their funds were sorely depleted and they had to borrow to pay their costs of £100.8s.4d. and counsel's fees of £117.7s.11d.

Undaunted by this failure they decided in 1839 to restart prosecuting encroachers, which the deacon's casting vote had stopped the year before. In 1843 they objected once more to the presence of tailors from other towns taking away their trade.[40] Another long fight with one, James Rodger, ended ignominiously for the Trade in 1846. Rodger had paid for a licence until 1839 when he was ordered to pay £33 to compensate for losses caused by his encroachments but in 1846 he claimed the Trade was not entitled to raise money in this way. It was noted that if the Murison case had been thought of the action might not have been brought.[41] In 1846 with the loss of all privileges imminent, judgement against privilege was logical.

While the Tailors were careful of their own rights, they were prepared to recognise those of other brethren. They agreed with the Bonnetmakers that they would stop making cloth bonnets in 1702 as this practice was considered unfair to the Trade whose living depended on these alone. A master tailor who broke the agreement was to be fined £10 Scots, a servant who independently did so lost £5 while one who did so under his master's orders was fined £15, which was divided equally between the Nine Trades, the Bonnetmakers and the Tailors.[42]

When times seemed to be hard the Tailors became worried about overmanning and took steps to restrict their numbers. In September 1655 the decision was taken not to admit masters or half-masters, an unexplained term, for seven years, except freeman's sons and sons-in-law and free apprentices. The same rule was repeated in February 1685 at a court of the Trade meeting in the New Kirk yard with the qualification that if their numbers were so depleted by the death of masters that they could not serve the lieges in the burgh, then they would countenance breaking this statute. Anyone who objected to this rule was liable to be fined.[43] Almost twenty years later in 1704 the 'frequent receaving of unfreemen' as freemasters was blamed for the 'losses of years bygone' and once again these restrictions in entry were imposed. Those who had served as apprentice to a freemaster were excepted from this restriction. The implication must be that all the others had not necessarily done so.

Like all the Dundee craftsmen by the end of the eighteenth century the Tailors were in favour of political reform. They collected for a fund to support burgh reform in 1819 and unanimously approved a petition to the House of Lords in 1831 approving the Reform Bill.[44] Strangely enough they do not seem to have discussed the act removing their privileges that was so momentous in its implications for all Trades. They were perhaps too absorbed in their own small battles. After the event, however, they apparently immediately divided up their funds among existing members and this action caused some acrimony. The news spread and claims were sent in by members, including a widow, Mrs Helen Young, who thought she should have her husband's share and demanded an *explicit* (*sic*) answer about her claim. If no amicable arrangement was reached she would consider she should have a full share.[45] Like most of the other Trades the Tailors continued dividing surplus funds among members thereafter.[46]

The incorporation had had financial problems to settle at various times in their history before this date. The collection of meal money was regularly a source of acrimony, but all the Trades were faced with backsliding members on that account. In the 1770s there seems to have been quite a lot of confusion. To start with, in 1771 deacon and boxmaster were forbidden to borrow money without the Trade's permission.[47] The next year it was agreed that though the officials had broken this rule a £10 debt must be honoured, lest the reputation of the Tailors or any other of the incorporated Trades suffered through its not being repaid.[48] The two officials concerned were censured for their bad management and were never to be allowed to serve again.

When we read in August 1773 that the boxmaster was to have no more than 5s. to his credit, it does not appear that the management can have improved. In 1775 a successor, James Duncan, 'had gone into confusion' in managing the Trade's affairs, collecting revenue and meal money without records. He was due £26.0s.5d. and was imprisoned before he repaid some of the money. As he had none left, the remainder was to be returned at the rate of £1.10s. per annum without interest until the balance was paid, an arrangement that speaks volumes for the sense and compassion of the Trade.[49]

Funds were to be boosted in 1779 when the 'entertainment' given by new freemasters was converted into an extra sum to the funds of £1.10s. and 7s.6d. for the new hall,[50] but there was still a problem. When Scottish drinking habits at funerals in the eighteenth century are remembered, one realises just how worried members must have been about the Trade's impecuniousness on seeing the decision of July 1787.[51] All members were bound by their own bye-laws to attend funerals of their brethren Tailors and fines were imposed on absentees. It had been the practice for members to meet and have their own wake using the fine money for their drinks. In future these fines were to go to the boxmaster for the benefit of the Trade. In 1809 funerals provided yet another possible source of funds, when a 6d. fine was imposed on any member not wearing black or decent apparel.[52]

In 1800, an attempt was made to keep the quarterly accounts in a more orderly form by buying a book specially to record these payments and making the point that all must pay. There was also the decision already mentioned to prosecute those not paying journeymen's booking money, though that was cancelled two months later.[53] More troubles were to come when John Frewin, boxmaster in 1816, refused 'in the most impertinent manner' to bring in the Trade's book.[54] No wonder they expressed 'vehemently' their indignation at the *contemptuous* and *improper treatment* they had received from him!

The calls on their funds arising from the 1819 quarrel among the Nine Trades did not help. They had to borrow £60 towards their costs in 1822.[55] And of course, their own legal fights against those such as Murison who were trying to practise their craft in the burgh did not improve their finances. Nor did the recalcitrance of yet another boxmaster who refused to attend meetings in the hall. When threatened with losing all benefits of membership he eventually agreed to carry out his duties, but in the meantime, the Trade had had problems in finding ready money for their poor.

In 1846 they had to borrow to pay legal fees and their share of rebuilding the South Church. £600 was the sum suggested.[56] They decided to sell their sittings in 1873 for £100.[57] Despite these difficulties they were not without resources, having property in various parts of the town bringing in rent and available as security. In 1864 they borrowed £750 on such security 'for purposes of the Trade', unspecified.[58] It is difficult to avoid the conclusion that it was their management that was at fault, or their choice of boxmasters. And perhaps it is not surprising that a rule was made in 1809 that anyone who would not accept the position of boxmaster had to pay £10.[59] When James Dick had refused to serve in 1799, he was told that he was liable for any damage arising from his action.[60]

All through the Trade's records one senses the members' concern that their pensioners should not suffer. In 1803 unfree masters had to pay £8.6s.8d., free apprentices £5 and free entrants £2. Two years later such concern saw these sums increased to £30, £20 and £8 for freemasters' sons, £10 for sons-in-law. In 1826 the question of what should be paid by relatives who were not 'handicrafts' was discussed in September.[61] It was suggested that their entry fee should be two thirds of that paid by the unfree. The fee was in fact raised to £50, not surprisingly in light of their legal expenses. It is also hardly surprising that one freemaster's son offered to pay the interest on the capital he would have needed to join, so that he could practise for a year, but this offer was refused.

The Trade's view of its financial state was so gloomy that a contribution to the new public seminaries was refused and the small donation of £1.1s. to the Orphan Institute was discontinued in 1833.[62] The first refusal was on the grounds that the funds were not held for such a purpose but the second did not mince matters; they were having to reduce their poor list because of the state of their funds.

The high cost of entry did not deter seventeen masters from joining between 1820 and 1830 but only three more names appear in the Lockit Book before 1846, the last in 1838. At the end of one minute book a list of members on 12 January 1846 contains 20 names.[63] Thereafter it looked as if the Trade was doomed. The next new masters were honorary members, Sir John Ogilvie of Inverquharity and David Baxter, honoured by all the Nine Trades in 1862 for their services to the town. It was 1871 before two more ordinary freemasters' names were entered in the Book, one a tailor's son, the other a clothier's. From 1889 until after the Second World War only 21 joined and not all were tailors. One was an electrical engineer, another a Newcastle coal merchant. At one time active members were so few that the Trade held its meetings in Tayport, at the home of the clerk, James Simpson, a Dundee solicitor.

From 1947 to November 1981 61 masters were entered in the Lockit Book, several described simply as gentlemen and the deacon in 1947 was W.S. Goodfellow, who was of course a baker to trade. In 1975 there was a suggestion that the Trade should be open to any wanting to join, whether connected with the clothing trade or not. Their numbers were declining and the fear was expressed that the Trade might become extinct.[64] No new entrants had appeared by November 1980 when the news that the Lockit Book needed repairs costing £250 pointed the need for funds. In May 1981 there was indignation that their numbers had been given by the Nine Trades as seven when they declared there were in fact 27 members.[65] However in June and November of that year the numbers were boosted by twelve new entrants, a welcome addition to the incorporation's numbers but there must still be room for concern, if a steady flow of new members cannot be sustained.

NOTES

[1] DDARC, GD/TD/T5.6.

[2] NT5.2.1.

[3] DDARC, GD/TD/T5.47.

[4] Warden, 1872, 229.

[5] Ibid., 421, 422.

[6] DDARC, GD/TD/T3.1.

[7] DDARC, GD/TD/T1.2, 8.11.1800.

[8] DDARC, GD/TD/T1.1, 20.1.1801.

[9] DDARC, GD/TD/T5.2. Modernised spelling is given here.

[10] DDARC, GD/TD/T5.3.

[11] Maxwell, 1891, 335.

[12] DDARC, GD/TD/T5.12.

[13] DDARC, GD/TD/T5.5.

[14] Maxwell, 1884, 303.

[15] DDARC, GD/TD/T5.7.

[16] DDARC, GD/TD/T5.8.

[17] DDARC, GD/TD/T5.12.

[18] DDARC, GD/TD/T5.14.

[19] DDARC, GD/TD/T5.9, 11.

[20] DDARC, GD/TD/T6.10.

[21] DDARC, GD/TD/T5.10.

[22] DDARC, GD/TD/T6.6, 11, 12, 13.

[23] DDARC, GD/TD/T1.1, 2.1.1765.

[24] Ibid., 19.9.1785.

[25] Ibid., 3.6.1790.

[26] Ibid., 14.6.1790.

[27] Ibid., 29.12.1790.

[28] DDARC, GD/TD/T2.2, 8.6.1812.

[29] DDARC, GD/TD/T1.1, 1.3.1802.

[30] DDARC, GD/TD/T1.2, 2.8.1819.

[31] Ibid., 23.7.1819.

[32] DDARC, GD/TD/T1.3, 5.2.1834.

[33] DDARC, GD/TD/T1.1, 16.6.1829.

[34] DDARC, GD/TD/T5.18.

[35] Ibid., 28.

[36] DDARC, GD/TD/T1.1, 8.5.1767.

[37] Ibid., May to June 1829.

[38] DDARC, GD/TD/T5.30.

[39] DDARC, GD/TD/T1.1, 5.12.1836.

[40] DDARC, GD/TD/T1.4, 4.6.1838; 1.10.1839; 18.5.1843.

[41] DDARC, GD/TD/T5.39.

[42] DDARC, GD/TD/T6.26.

[43] TLB.

[44] DDARC, GD/TD/T1.2, 27.5.1819; 21.9.1831.

[45] DDARC, GD/TD/T4.7–13.

[46] DDARC, GD/TD/T1.5, 22.11.1882.

[47] DDARC, GD/TD/T1.1, p. 22.

[48] Ibid., 20.6.1772.

[49] Ibid., 31.3.1775.

[50] Ibid., 22.6.1779.

[51] Ibid., 30.7.1787.

[52] Ibid., 1809.

[53] Ibid., 28.11.1800.

[54] DDARC, GD/TD/T1.2, 5.7.1816.

[55] Ibid., 28.11.1822.

[56] DDARC, GD/TD/T1.4, 27.7.1846.

[57] DDARC, GD/TD/T1.5, 9.12.1873.

[58] Ibid., 3.6.1864.

[59] DDARC, GD/TD/T1.1, 20.2.1809.

[60] Ibid., p. 107.

[61] DDARC, GD/TD/T1.2, 13.9.1826.

[62] DDARC, GD/TD/T1.1, 8.10.1833; 16.12.1833.

[63] DDARC, GD/TD/T1.3, 12.1.1846.

[64] DDARC, GD/TD/T2.2, November 1975.

[65] Ibid., May 1981.

5. BONNETMAKER TRADE BANNER, ST ANDREW'S CHURCH

(Spanphoto, Dundee)

CHAPTER 8

The Bonnetmaker Trade

The Bonnetmaker Trade possesses two Seals of Cause, the first dated 31 July 1496, the second 28 September 1525.[1] The usual format is observed in the first. The provost, bailies and council of the burgh allow the Trade to set up an altar in Our Lady Kirk, this one in honour of St Bride, and to elect a deacon to keep order in the craft, as other craftsmen did 'in this good town'. The council also ratified the rules already proposed by the craft for its own good governance. This would seem yet another example of a craft that had been operating as a society with its own rules before its recognition by the council.

Almost thirty years later, in the second Seal of Cause the wording regarding the altar is slightly different. It is 'to be foundit'. Perhaps the Bonnetmakers had not yet achieved their earlier plan to help beautify the great town kirk. As most of the sums for entry fees and fines are increased in the new arrangement, it may be that financial stringency had prevented the Trade from providing St Bride with an altar. A new master in 1496 paid one merk (13s.4d.) and one pound of wax to the altar, 6s.8d. if he was a burgess' son. In 1525 this went up to 40s., two pounds of wax to the 'saintly light', their patron saint's altar, and another to Our Lady Light, the kirk itself.

The Trade's current Lockit Book has entered masters since 1965. It is very handsomely bound in black leather decorated with brass. Its predecessor opened on 11 August 1660 with the statement that their 'old and ancient book' had been lost when General Monck stormed the burgh on 1 September 1651. Next the Craft piously noted down the names of as many of their predecessors as they could remember. This volume was rebound in 1777 by James Mores for 4s.6d.[2] and in 1871, a business notice embossed on the front cover endpaper tells us it was repaired by J.R. Brechin, a bookbinder in Castle Street. Pages have been misplaced, as usual in these circumstances, and now the first pages contain various ordinances made later than the earliest entry, the first dated 31 October 1668.

Among the Bonnetmakers' records is a volume, wooden bound, the wood covered with leather, which must cast doubts on the 1660 statement that the Trade's Lockit Book was lost in 1651. A decorative panel is stamped on both back and front. This is a method of binding used in Scotland in the sixteenth century. The wood is worm-eaten and the back cover is broken, while the leather cover is so worn that it has lost most of its decorative tooling. Only a small part of the inscription on the panel is legible and a figure can just be seen holding something in his/her hands. On the cover there are the remains of metal locks. At the top of the cover, there is an inscription which must be a later addition as the panel is upside down in relation to this title. Partly worn away, it reads

IS IS THE BO
ET MAKERS BOOK.

Presumably 'Th' is missing from the first word and 'n' from Bonet. The whole would make up the usual wording on a Lockit Book.

It has been rebound at some time for some leather thongs remain attached to the cover but there are no corresponding holes in the paper while pieces of paper with some writing on them have been used to strengthen the spine. The first regulation by date is the earliest entry in the book. It records a decree of the Craft of 28 July 1541 that no apprentice was to be taken on without being entered in the book, 'signed and received by the whole brethren and masters' and 10s. being paid to the deacon. Then follows a list of over twenty names headed by David Hog, deacon. It is not possible to be precise about numbers as the ink is so faded and the page is worn at the edges.

From the next page onwards the entry of masters is recorded. 'The four score years an free master of the bonetmaker craft Patrick of Murray' comes first. This may mean a 1580 entry but we cannot be sure. The ink of the second on the page is very faint but it can be read with difficulty. It shows that Alexander Flechar became a master in July 1549, promising to be loyal and true to the Bonnetmaker Craft. There are then 26 entries of masters, the date 1589 given only on the first, all taking the oath to defend the welfare of the craft. Nineteen entries follow under 1590 and thereafter masters are regularly entered until 1657, eight between 1652 and that final date.

This must surely be the older Lockit Book that the 1660 craftsmen believed lost in 1651, though it has been rebound and had a title added that later craftsmen thought appropriate. One wonders how it was that the Trade's collective memory failed to remember these masters so recently entered as late as 1657. It is difficult to avoid the conclusion that the

Trade had simply mislaid their Lockit Book and produced this collective cover-up.

It cannot have been missing for long after 1660. In the book opened that year, there are pages of entries dating from the previous century written in one fine seventeenth century hand. These have undoubtedly been copied, though incompletely, from the 'old and ancient' book. The same names and dates occur though Alexander Flechar's date of entry is given as 1529. The 'remembered' names of 1660 correspond only slightly with the names on the copied list. Until 1708 the old and new Lockit Books were used apparently indiscriminately.

The Bonnetmakers' Lockit Books are no different from others in that they are not necessarily kept methodically, at least not by modern standards. In the older of the two the entry of masters and apprentices and undated accounts are mixed after 1642. The last five entries from 1713 to 1728 are free apprentices. On one of the first pages there are two notices: George Belye becomes a tenant of the craft in 1734 and James Miln gives his bond as cautioner for his mother-in-law's house rent in 1738.

At the back of the book financial matters dominate, dating from 1729, and from these entries we find that the Bonnetmakers let houses to ten tenants and also collected 'crop rent' until at least 1742 when William Addie paid £43. This evidence shows they must have owned land. Another small leather bound book recording rents shows they still had two acres of land in 1750. Andrew Langlands who collected the rents described himself as rentmaster, not boxmaster. Like the other trades with any considerable property the Bonnetmakers may have found it more efficient to separate the two functions. It was never an easy task with rests (arrears) figuring as regularly as rents. In 1744 George Billie, probably the George Belye mentioned above, paid six years arrears of rent; but at least he did pay.

Among the entries of masters from the sixteenth century a few rules are interspersed. In 1604 strangers coming into the burgh to work must report to the deacon and pay 10s. – 'incontinent'. No delay is allowed and the deacon is responsible to the craft in seeing this is done. A master who broke the rules was fined 2s. for every day he employed a servant without the deacon's consent. Another rule regarding servants in this volume dated 20 December 1559 ordained that any servant who went off to play or drink without his master's leave was to have no work for fourteen days – 'to gang idle' during that time, no doubt without pay, a hard punishment. Also servants who did not complete their weekly task lost their free Saturday evening.

It is mysterious that the Trade made no overt mention of having found this book when it was evidently in use. At least there is no record remaining of its rediscovery in the 1660 Lockit Book but there is no saying what might have happened in the rebinding. Even more mysterious is Warden's belief that the Bonnetmakers had no ancient documents. *The Burgh Laws* was published in 1872 and he stated quite categorically that the Bonnetmakers had no documents older than the 1660 Lockit Book. In 1858, only fourteen years before, an old kist had been opened and the clerk, Mr Rollo, had been asked to list all the papers found in it. The list produced on 27 September 1860 was engrossed in the minutes of that date and the documents were returned to the kist. These papers date from the early sixteenth century and contain many of vital importance to the Trade's privileges.[3]

Warden was a member of the Trade and deacon in the 1870s. He attended the first meeting recorded in the minute book that begins in 1861.[4] How had someone so interested in the history of Dundee and the Nine Trades missed such an important happening? Why had no-one told him about the old documents? Where was the kist when he worked on the Bonnetmakers' history?

There can be no doubt that the book just described is included among these documents. In the clerk's list, under number 9, the first thing mentioned is a 'Large old book'. Measuring 6″ × 8½″ × 1½″ it hardly merits being called a large volume but the contents are those of the one just described – allowing for a busy clerk's not taking time to decipher the earlier writing – 1589–1728, with rentals at the back. The loose papers still in the clerk's possession tally with the rest of Mr Rollo's inventory. Some of these documents will be referred to in the next few pages.

This treasure trove contains many sasines and charters referring to the properties in which craft funds had been invested, though there were some the clerk considered useless. The Trade owns copies and originals of acts, letters and agreements of various sorts, mostly in their favour. They retain copies of the 1556 charter by Mary of Guise, which confirmed the liberties of the crafts. But is seems to have lain forgotten until 1911. Then the Seals of Cause reappeared once again and at a meeting of 2 May that year the members present examined them with great interest. Where and by whom they had been found is not recorded but they seem to have lain in the several clerks' hands, most of the time forgotten and disregarded through four centuries.[5]

Like all the Trades, the free bonnetmakers were careful of their privileges, at least in the sixteenth and seventeenth centuries. It must have been more difficult for them than for some others even to pretend to exclusive rights and skills, at least in the making up of the bonnets, the 'wifing', i.e. weaving or knitting. Knitting is not the most esoteric of skills and as one author noted, it could be picked up without a long apprenticeship.[6] As early as 1521 one unfree worker had his work forfeited to the church.[7] This meant that at any time there were a great many people knitting bonnets quite skilfully with no regard for any of the craft regulations and undercutting the official prices no doubt followed.

Fortunately for the free bonnetmakers, knitting up the blue bonnets was only one part of the process. Preparation and dyeing of the blue woollen yarn used and fulling of the finished article were all equally important. The 1525 Seal of Cause ruled that the bonnetmaker who would actually work dyed wool must order it himself and further, that the dyer must be a local man. There was also concern about the quality of the dye used, and the Trade passed acts at intervals to try to ensure that Dundee bonnets were not treated with inferior dye-stuff. A deep strong blue was the preferred colour and it was produced satisfactorily only by woad.

What seem to have been the last two acts of the Trade to regulate the colour of bonnets were passed in 1694 and 1710.[8] The ordinance of 1694 expressed great worry about the damage done to the craft's reputation by the production of bonnets that were too light in colour, treated with 'bersill' – dye made from brazil wood – and alum. These were said to be 'a great cheat to the country and disgrace to ourselves'. To prevent such action in the future sacks of finished bonnets were to be sealed up at the waulkmill and only opened to allow them to be examined by 'secharchers' to ensure they were a good colour. Poor samples were taken to the deacon and the makers had to pay 13s.4d. before they were allowed to take the bonnets away. The examiners themselves were subject to a fine of 3s.4d. if they did not carry out this task properly. The later enactment of June 1710, laying on fines of 20s., increasing for repetition of the offence to 40s. and then to £3, seems to show that the first had not been wholly effective.

Fulling was a vitally important process in bonnetmaking. A proper bonnet could not be made without the work of the Waulkers who do not always seem to have worried about the privileges of the other incorporation. In the 1580s and perhaps before there had been a considerable threat to Dundee bonnetmakers from outside the burgh.[9] There had been a great increase in the number of unfree workers in the Hilltown and other places near there who were acting like free masters, 'using liberty as if they were free'. The Bonnetmaker Trade had complained 'most earnestly' to their fellow incorporation, the Waulkers, about the iniquity of their helping these unfreemen, for without their co-operation the unfree would have laboured in vain.

On 27 October 1589 the two crafts came to an agreement. For the 'great love' they bore the bonnetmakers, the waulkers would stop fulling for the unfree in the Hill or anywhere else. To compensate for the loss they would suffer from this self-denying ordinance, they were to receive half the fines imposed by the authorised craft on those unfree who encroached on their privileges. The solution of renting their own waulkmill must have removed some of the annoyance the Bonnetmakers experienced. The Trade rented the mill at Balmossie from the Panmure estate from the mid-seventeenth century. In 1671 £26 of silver duty was paid for it.[10] The mill had to be kept in good repair and the accounts show regular entries for materials and labour. The millwright was given a substantial 'perk', a bonnet. As the price in 1707 was 16s. that was a handsome addition to his wages.[11]

The Bonnetmakers employed their own waulker at the Balmossie mill. In March 1724 a special meeting was called to place a 'sufficient workman' there and as the existing tenant, William Scot, was deemed satisfactory he was kept on. The tenant had to provide a horse and cart daily to carry unwaulked bonnets to the mill to be fulled and to return the finished articles back to Dundee. Previously a horse and cart would have been hired by the Trade, and at 6s. for a horse when bonnets in numbers in excess of 20,000 were being carried back and forwards that expense would have been considerable.[12] Bonnets gradually went out of fashion during the eighteenth century and the number of makers decreased so much that by the 1780s the mill was no longer necessary.[13]

Another craft on whom bonnetmakers depended was that of the skinners who provided the wool for their yarn. The Dundee Skinners were taken to court by their fellow craftsmen in the burgh for using 'false and diverse' measures and weights for several years past, to their own benefit of course. This was contrary to several acts of the Scottish parliament that throughout the country these should be the same. Despite these acts, it was in fact long after the union of 1707 before such desirable uniformity came into being. The Bonnetmaker Trade were particularly annoyed that the Skinners did not even use the 'common measure of Dundee'. The Court of Session accepted the realities of the situation and, the act of the three Estates notwithstanding, on 20 June 1611 the judges ordered skinners to sell their wool in the future according to the weights of the Dundee weighhouse.[14]

Despite the thousands of bonnets which were waulked, at 1d. a time, there seem to be very few genuine old models now in existence. No instructions for making them appear in any detail in the records. Contracts with servants mention differentiation between tasks of spinning, 'dichting' (dressing) and weaving (knitting).[15] There were variations in skills. Not all

128

servants seem to have been able to make bonnets from start to finish, at least in their masters' eyes. In 1672 when the Trade was in debt, one method used to increase their funds was to demand extra payment of 2s.2d. as well as the usual quarterly accounts for more skilled servants who could dicht bonnets.[16]

The only descriptions of bonnets given in the Trade's archive are by weight and size and these appear only in the agreements made when a journeyman was hired.[17] Both men and women servants made these agreements. Sometimes the weight refers to the yarn that has to be worked, sometimes it is the bonnet's weight that is specified. In January 1693 Janet Hog agreed to work 13 pounds of yarn weekly for £8 a year and a sark, a shift or chemise. Twenty-four bonnets of ten ounces were the task of another servant in 1694 while in 1683 Andrew Mill was allowed a week to work fourteen bonnets of the six pound sort or seventeen of four pound.

These weights must refer to the type of yarn for a six pound bonnet would be too much for any head! The yarn too had to have sufficient till, i.e. to have enough strands spun into the yarn. Sizes are vague. 'Little' and 'middling' are hardly precise measurements, though by the 1730s size numbers are given. Such terms as common and fine bonnets and 'mangler' or 'mangrel' (mixed) appear, which to the contemporary craftsmen and women obviously needed no definition.

Though the bonnets needed the co-operation of various trades, brotherly love did not often appear to stop one incorporated craft from undercutting or cheating another, at least not without some recompense. There was at least one exception in the history of the Bonnetmakers. As we saw, the Tailor Trade in 1702 promised to stop making cloth bonnets, which would be produced faster than those knitted by bonnetmakers. In a remarkable show of labour solidarity, the tailors admitted that making bonnets of cloth was unfair to the other craft.[18]

Like all the other incorporated trades, the Bonnetmakers tried to protect themselves against any unfairness as they saw it. They tried to stop any trading by those who were not members of the society. As well as passing their own acts, they enrolled other authorities whenever possible, including the Court of Session, as we have seen. In 1572, the town council allowed for the confiscation of the goods of any unfree workmen and of forestallers who traded illegally in bonnets. Half of the escheated goods went to the king, the other to the common works of the burgh, not the Trade. Any freeman who joined in partnership with one of these unfree was to lose his own liberty, his privilege as a freeman.

The incorporation benefited from James VI's warrant in February 1593

(1594 by today's reckoning) in favour of the Trade. The king pointed out that unfree craftsmen in the suburbs caused great damage by encouraging servants to leave their masters as they could find work there. The forfeiture of the goods of the unfree who might 'traduce' was authorised. The craft decided to publicise this letter for they thought that ignorance of its contents caused them great harm.[19]

In the early eighteenth century another practice was damaging the burgh's bonnet trade. Members of the Trade were buying Glasgow bonnets and passing them off as the work of local makers, selling them even in Dundee itself. This threat to the Dundee craft could not go unnoticed. On 13 October 1726 the Trade forbade this, imposing a large fine of £3 Scots for the first offence, to be doubled each time the offence was repeated. Dundee merchants were buying these bonnets and it is implied that they knew well that their purchases were not Dundee made. To help maintain their monopoly the Dundee craft ordered their members, and members' widows and children to refrain from selling any bonnets at all to merchants whom the Trade convicted of buying Glasgow bonnets.[20]

Most of the rules referring to the privileges granted to the various trade incorporations had to be repeated, but this enactment like the 1710 order concerning dyeing does not seem to reappear. It would not be safe to assume that therefore they had been effective in light of the decrease in the craft as fashion overtook it. The Trades who were most active in the eighteenth century in fighting for their monopolistic privileges were usually those who were prospering in their historic crafts.

In one respect there is some evidence that the Bonnetmaker Trade was unique in the burgh. Alone among the incorporated trades, the Bonnetmakers do not seem to have insisted on freemasters' becoming burgesses, even before the decline of the craft, despite the insistence on such a condition in both Seals of Cause. Indeed in the 1660 Lockit Book we find the peculiar rule, peculiar that is for a Trade incorporation, that any of the craft who bragged of his burgess-ship to his neighbour would be fined 40s.

This regulation may well imply that becoming a burgess was an extra status symbol for a bonnetmaker. In all the other Dundee Trades becoming a burgess was an essential step to entry; it would not have been necessary to brag about it. There is no date attached to the entry and its position in the book between two entries of 1608 and 1647 makes it almost impossible to say when the Trade passed this statute. James Barie's name as deacon is at the head of the entry but the practice of writing in the name of the deacon in this way happened at different times. We find it during the 1620s for instance; then it stopped and started, but unfortunately Barie's name makes its only appearence here.

Another of the Trade's acts[21] of 27 May 1674 lays down a rule which seems to give some strength to the belief that becoming a free burgess was not essential. The bonnetmakers are certainly out of line with the regulations of any other Trade. The significant phrase is that 'No free man to our Trade and not free to the burgh' (my underlining) shall use burgess liberty in buying bonnets, dressed or undressed. The fines imposed were 40s. for the first transgression, £4 for the second and loss of liberty for the third. Such wording surely shows that a master bonnetmaker could be a member of the Trade without paying for his burgess ticket, though he would not be able to share in all the benefits.

The practice presumably continued, for in the nineteenth century there was trouble on at least one occasion over the elections of magistrates. On 23 September 1819 twelve bonnetmakers attended the meeting to elect the town's magistrates. Deacon William Hogg and two other members were not allowed to vote. The reason given was that either they had not become burgesses or they had simply declined to show their burgess tickets. The boxmaster noted that apart from their not being burgesses they had not paid their dues and were ineligible under these circumstances too.[22] It was pointed out that it was the town council's rule that only burgesses could take part when the Trade elected magistrates.

William Hogg was clearly a rumbustious, agressive character, one in a long list of Hoggs who had figured in the Trade's history. He was prepared to stand up for the Trade's rights without fear or favour – where they did not conflict with his – but sometimes went too far for his brethren's tastes. In 1807,[23] the Nine Trades informed the Bonnetmakers that they would not accept him as their representative until he apologised for his irregular and disorderly behaviour at meetings. Sometimes his fellow craftsmen agreed with him as in September 1817 when he protested at the town council meeting that everything done there was illegal. His grounds for this contention were that he received notice only at 10 a.m. for 12 noon and therefore could not call the Trade. They were less happy with him the following year.

In June he had interrupted the Provost's formal signing of a petition to the Convention of Royal Burghs. This time he objected to the method of appointing the Convener of the Nine Trades because the Trades were not to have power to elect their own councillors. As the Trade had instructed him differently, they recorded their disapproval in the minutes and sent a transcript to the town council.[24]

He roused more disapproval in the months following. At a meeting called by his request on 7 November 1818 when he was to hand over the Trade's books, he arrived late and refused 'perempterly' to give them up. The Bonnetmakers decided to take legal steps against him. He left the room when a meeting of 12 July 1819 decided that the present deacon and box-master should keep the keys of the Lockit Book. His next step was to raise a summons against Deacon Leslie on account of the vote of censure the Trade had passed against him. Not surprisingly, Leslie was allowed to use the Craft's funds as it was considered Hogg was acting against the Trade generally.

Hogg's lawsuit, however tiresome it must have seemed to the deacon and boxmaster named in the summons, was overshadowed by the 1819 dispute between the smaller and the larger Trades. The Bonnetmakers refused to become actively involved in this dispute in any way, because they were so divided themselves. While Deacon Leslie wanted to take part with the majority, others in the incorporation were completely opposed to this. In the end, non-participation was the only answer. Despite this decision, the minutes of their meetings are full of references to the case, with regular responses to letters from the convener to the effect that the whole affair had nothing to do with them, or that they were not willing to pay any part of the cost of the case.

It is difficult to avoid the impression that the Trade felt slightly remote by this time from the interests of the other eight. No other Trade had become so divorced from its origins. The other members of the Nine Trades were all still involved in producing some form of the goods that their predecessors in the burgh had made. The Bonnetmaker Craft was in a different position. For centuries it would seem that every man and boy wore a bonnet, and the craft had an insatiable market. Fashions changed however and different types of headgear became the norm for men, but bonnetmakers did not change with them. They did not apparently try to alter their patterns or methods to accommodate new fashions. Nor do their own existing records give any inkling that they ever considered turning their skills to making other sorts of knitted garments.

With an almost obsolete craft as the reason for the very existence of the incorporation and the change of emphasis in the enrolment of members to the society, the Bonnetmaker Trade did not always react to events as the other eight did. For instance, much to the horror of the Nine Trades as a whole, they sold their share in St Andrew's, the Trades Kirk, to the Kirk Session. So of course did the Dyers who were somewhat at odds with the others at the time. The Nine Trades bought both shares back as soon as they could. In these circumstances too, it was not to be expected that the Bonnet-makers would show much interest in fighting for trade liberties in the nineteenth century.

New members had joined the society regularly throughout the eighteenth century, 16 between 1761, when George Dempster was made an honorary member, and 1784. This throws some doubts on one estimate that there were only four members around the latter date[25] unless this meant that there were only four men among the members who actually made bonnets. It was only from 11 March 1790 that occupations other than bonnetmaking were regularly attributed to new entrants in the Lockit Book, though earlier in 1768 the Alexander Beveridge entry noted his profession as writer. This instance was not necessarily significant as all the Trades tended to enrol writers, often their clerk, and sometimes as 'dry-handed' member. Dry-handed is a term that I have not found in the Bonnetmakers' records and that in itself may indicate than men of very diverse trades and professions had been joining the society in numbers for some time.

Four men joined in March 1790. One was the redoubtable William Hogg, then 'Junior', who was a merchant and the son of a merchant. His fellow entrants included a second merchant, William Spence, a surgeon's son; a stocking weaver, William Leslie; and the bookseller, Edward Leslie, Hogg's later opponent in the Trade, who was the son of a shipmaster. Significantly, all of these men were made freemasters 'in right of their respective fathers', who had certainly not earned their living making bonnets.

On 6 May that year, however, two new masters entered whose occupations were given as bonnetmakers. John Martin was the son and John Powrie the son-in-law of freemen whose occupations were not stated. It has been claimed that the last practising bonnetmaker was enrolled in 1790. Either Martin or Powrie or both could qualify but it is impossible to be sure from the Trade records alone. Until 1790 all masters were entered as bonnetmakers including people such as Provost Alexander Riddoch and George Dempster of Dunnichen, who was made a member or honorary member of all the Dundee Trades. It is wellnigh impossible to know before then who were and who were not practising craftsmen; there were probably very few. According to one writer[26] there was only one bonnetmaker knitting in the traditional way in the early nineteenth century who had died in 1848.

The Trade's total silence in their nineteenth century records regarding the threat to Trade privileges even before 1832 can come as no surprise. Even the 1846 act was passed with no comment. What to its modern members in more democratic days may seem more reprehensible, and considering the atmosphere in Dundee at the time, somewhat unusual, is the apparent lack of interest in burgh reform. In June 1819 a contribution towards sending a delegate to the House of Commons committee on burgh reform was refused and five years later in 1824 there was no support for an action proposed by other Dundee groups for action on the set of the burgh.[27] Parliamentary reform on the other hand did receive some support and in September 1831 the Trade sent a petition to Lord Panmure asking him to present it to the House of Lords. In this they asked that the Reform Bill should be passed by the upper house.

The views of the membership or at least of those who were most active in the incorporation at the time must have been reflected in such decisions. These views must have been very varied. Alexander Riddoch, generally but not universally held up as the prime figure of burgh corruption in Dundee,[28] became a master in 1789. Eight years later Alexander Robertson's stand when he became a member demonstrates the radical freethinking proclivities of many Dundonians of the time. He refused to take an oath with any religious content or one giving any promise of obedience to the magistrates and town council, and was accepted on his own terms.

The entrants' oath in most crafts swore fealty to Christianity. After the Reformation this was sometimes carefully qualified with the words 'as presently professed', as in the earliest written example of the oath of the Bonnetmakers so far found,[29] but all had a religious element. Obedience was also promised to the king, the provost and bailies and to the deacon. At the back of the 1660 Lockit Book there is a more modern version written in an eighteenth century hand. Since Alexander Robertson's stand on 28 September 1797, would-be freemasters of the Bonnetmaker Trade need promise only to be peaceable members of society and of the craft, promoting its interests and that of its widows and orphans.

It was 17 October 1832 before the incorporation declared itself officially an open one, i.e. one which 'all who wish to practise the art or trade of Bonnet making' could join.[30] After that date new members needed only to profess the aspiration to skill, not to demonstrate it. The instructions to the deacon and a committee to publicise this decision showed that the men who had made it knew exactly what they meant to make of the Society. Opening the incorporation officially to all, and becoming in effect a social club was only honest. More formal rules were made in January 1861 when it was decided that prospective members must write and request membership.

With a current membership of over 300, the old craft society of Bonnetmakers is today a social club for men of many trades and professions, but there can be little doubt that members are aware and proud of their history.

It is interesting that the deacon had no chain of office until 1860 and it was in 1913 that the proposal to present retiring deacons with a gold badge was accepted. The flag or banner however was shown throughout the Craft's long history on all appropriate occasions and repaired or renewed as the Trade thought fit. It was flown on seven occasions, for example in 1747–48 at a cost of 14s.[31] and renewed most recently in 1966.[32]

All new entrants to the Trade receive a copy of Rev. T.R.S. Campbell's history of their craft which serves to remind them of its place in Dundee's past. The translations of the two Seals of Cause by another bonnetmaker, Mr Iain Flett, Dundee District Archivist, help them to understand the standards and beliefs of their predecessors. The men who set up their society of practising bonnetmakers so many centuries ago might have difficulty in recognising their incorporation as it operates today but there can be little doubt that the freemasters of 1832 made a realistic decision. Later generations of Dundonians have demonstrated their approval by joining the society with enthusiasm.

NOTES

[1] The clerk of the Trade, Mr Tweedie, has custody of all the Trade's records except the two Seals of Cause which are kept by the Trade's bank.

[2] BmTAB.

[3] BmT Sederent (sic) Book, 1817–1861. 27.9.1860. Hereafter BmTSB.

[4] BmTMB, 1861–1946.

[5] BmTMB, 2.5.1911.

[6] W.C. Skinner, M.A., The Barronie of Hilltowne (Dundee, 1927), 32.

[7] Maxwell, 1891, 334.

[8] BmTAB.

[9] BmT, Bundle 8 includes all the documents relevant to this case.

[10] BmT, Small leather rent book.

[11] BmTAB.

[12] Ibid., 1707.

[13] T.R.S. Campbell, A Short History of the Bonnetmaker Craft (1987). Hereafter Campbell, 1987.

[14] BmT, Bundle 8.

[15] BmTAB.

[16] BmTLB, 20.12.1672.

[17] BmTAB.

[18] See the chapter on the Tailors for this episode.

[19] BmT, Bundle 8.

[20] BmTAB, p. 48.

[21] BmT, Bundle 8.

[22] BmTSB, 23.9.1819.

[23] NT2.5, 20.5.1807.

[24] BmTSB, p. 29, 30.6.1818.

[25] Campbell, 1987, 6.

[26] Millar, 1925, 37.

[27] BmTSB, 3.6.1819; 10.11.1824.

[28] See Gauldie, 1989, for a different view.

[29] BmTLB, 1660 eighth page.

[30] BmTSB, 17.10.1832.

[31] BmTAB, 1747–48. ·

[32] Campbell, 1987.

CHAPTER 9

The Flesher Trade

As a result of the unfortunate theft of their records[1] the history of the in-corporation of Fleshers must necessarily be defective. The Trade ranks sixth among the Nine. One clue to the date of the Trade's Seal of Cause appears in the 'Inventory and Abbreviary of ye Toune of Dundie – Charters and Sealls of Causes' dated 1711, to be found in the archive of the Nine Trades.[2] The entry referring to the Fleshers is written in a more modern hand than the first recorded Seals of Cause and is numbered 13 in the inventory. According to this entry the date of the 'Sale of Cause' granted in favour of the Fleshers of Dundie was 3 April 1495 when William Mitchell was deacon. The entry in the Inventory states that the Seal of Cause was given in favour of the Fleshers of Dundee by the deacon with the consent of the *ministers*, provost, baillies and council of the burgh. Possibly the eight-eenth century clerk mistook an abbreviation for masters in the original and thought that a minister was bound to have been present in any such transaction.

Though the Lockit Book of the Trade is missing, Fleshers appear in other records but as individuals, rather than as members of their incorporation. Fleshers, dyers and shoemakers were discriminated against in the Laws of the Four Burghs which enacted that butchers might not become guild members in any burgh unless they handed over the actual working of their craft to servants.[3] This rule was on account of the nature of their work, which tended to stain their hands, making them look perpetually dirty.

In Dundee itself regulations about the way butchers should practise their craft appear in the town council minutes. On 9 September 1642 the town council agreed unanimously that they could keep their crans on the street on market days as they had in the past. This rule was qualified by the condition that the privilege was at the council's pleasure and was followed by the order that fleshers were to obey the council's acts about keeping the streets clean. This cannot have been an easy task with only well water available.

The additional instruction that they were to take no part in 'breaking' any meat brought in by butchers from outside the burgh might also have been aimed at street cleanliness as well as protecting the liberties of the burgess fleshers. If traders from outside the burgh slaughtered and cut up their animals before they came to market, there would be less mess on the Dundee causeways. In the days before the town had an official abattoir this process must have resulted in a considerable amount of unpleasant and malodorous refuse. Dundee town council regularly showed great concern about the state of the burgh's streets, though in the conditions of earlier centuries they were probably fighting a losing battle.[4] The need to impose a fine on anyone who hamstrung cattle or let them stand bleeding on the road gives an inkling of conditions in the early part of the sixteenth century.[5]

We can also find the names of some earlier butchers or fleshers in lists of burgesses of the burgh of Dundee. Almost certainly those practising the trade who became freemen of the burgh would also join the incorporation. The Flesher Trade was never a very large one in the town so when we find four Barries gaining their freedom between 1556 and 1570 and even more Constables, twelve in all from 1631 to 1723, seven of these between 1645 and 1662, all described as butchers or fleshers, it is reasonable to assume that their families must have been prominent in the incorporation.[6] Unfortunately, without the Trade's own records, only informed guesswork is possible.

The first privilege belonging to freemen of the Trade would be the obvious one of controlling the sale of meat in the burgh but in Dundee the local Trade had a particular place. The Flesher Trade was in charge of the town shambles, where 'killing houses' were rented out to members, and they also controlled the yard where the animals stood before they were slaughtered. In 1560 a 'fleshhouse' had been built on the west side of the Castle Burn 'where the myddings are', extra taxation being levied for the purpose.[7] The stones of the Grey Friars monastery were to be used and the town council sensibly decided that the Flesher Craft should have most say in the design.[8] In theory all animals brought into Dundee to be butchered should have been slaughtered there.

Like all the incorporated Trades, the Fleshers tried to maintain their monopoly over their trade, without complete success. They laid down rules for the selling of meat and for the management of the shambles. Carcases brought in from outside the burgh were treated differently though still incurring charges. Any man who did not bring all his meat to the market to sell, for instance, could be in trouble. So was a butcher who brought unsatisfactory meat to market, whether a member of the Craft or not.

'Blowing' carcases, presumably to make them look larger, or selling meat from diseased animals could lead to the forfeiture of the seller's goods.[9]

'Killing house' was the term always used for the slaughterhouses in the earlier records and until the loss of burgh and trade privileges non-members, the unfree, were not allowed to rent these premises in the shambles. Many of these rents were more often in arrears than not, but the shambles still provided an income for the Trade for its poor fund and for any repairs and improvements needed there. Butchers had to pay for each beast killed in the town or brought in and there was also profit from the blood and manure necessarily produced. This money was considered the property of the Trade not of the individual tradesmen. From 1784 all new entrants were bound to take all possible care to preserve the blood and dung of all bestial slaughtered, because of the benefit the sale of those by-products brought to the poor of the Trade.[10]

The income so generated grew steadily from the eighteenth to the mid-nineteenth century. The Sugar House bought the blood for the year 1782–83 for £6 when the dung was also rouped for £8, but in 1846 these sums had grown to £55 offered for blood[11] and £153 for dung.[12] By that time the Fleshers needed every penny, as we shall see, and the income from these by-products of their trade helped keep their creditors at bay.

The incorporation's responsibility for keeping the shambles in good order and undertaking repairs and improvements could mean increased charges. For instance on 23 October 1714, to recoup the cost of four new doors costing £100 Scots the Trade increased the amount a flesher had to pay for slaughtering an ox, cow, calf or pig to 12d. from 8d. while the price for each sheep, lamb and goat was doubled from 2d. to 4d. (all Scots money). At the same time, fleshers were ordered not to conceal any bestial they had slain.

It was not always easy to supply only good meat in healthy condition to the burgesses. On the same day that the Trade set these higher prices, their records note that the inhabitants of the burgh were accusing the fleshers of 'blowing' meat. A fine of 40s. was proposed for the first offence, £3 for the second and £3 plus the confiscation of the beast for the third. This punishment was to be imposed not on the master or servant found committing this crime but on the master at the door of whose killing-house it was done, on the grounds that he must have at least connived in the action. It was hardly a process that could be carried out secretly within the shambles precincts.

The watchman at the shambles was the first person to guard the quality of meat. He had to report any doubtful cases to members of the Trade whether the animals in question had been slaughtered there or were carcases

138

brought in from landward areas. The watchman was also responsible for keeping order in the yard. Animals were not always slaughtered immediately and this delay could cause trouble. In the spring of 1845 the lessee of the dung complained of the damage done by a 'gang of pigs' owned by Messrs Niven, and the boxmaster was empowered to erect a rail to enclose these marauders.[13]

Some years later the Trade faced a different, unwelcome and new type of criticism. The Police Commissioners complained that it had been reported that there was no proper shelter for bestial waiting to be slaughtered and further that they sometimes stood for days without food or water. The Trade, not unnaturally, were not prepared to acknowledge such a state of affairs. Their answer was that it did not pay butchers to let animals suffer, but at the same time, the deacon and boxmaster were told to arrange for more shelter for cattle.[14]

In 1714, the earliest record the Trade possesses shows that the Fleshers called themselves 'Masters of the Shambles'.[15] They may have been claiming such a title before that date. In fact they were merely tenants of the town council, regularly paying a rent – £5 for 1764–65.[16] The shambles built in 1560 was in the very heart of the burgh and like the later 'Pillars' seems to have been a meeting place for the inhabitants. One of the doors of the shambles, that on the north side facing the High Street, was referred to in 1720 as one of the five principal places in the burgh.[17] The Flesher Trade was responsible for the upkeep of the buildings and yard but significantly the council kept control of the ground on which they were built.

The Trade discovered how little they were in fact 'masters' when the town council decided to alter the town's streets in one of their early improvement schemes in 1770. The Fleshers were outraged when they first heard the news. They fought a rearguard action, protesting that the new venue proposed would be much less convenient for them. On 22 May 1770 their minute book records that fifteen masters objected to the town council's summons to remove, and they agreed to apply to the Court of Session. The Court's decision could only go against them, and the Trade eventually had no real option but to accept the situation. They had to move slightly further away from the town centre to the west side of the Greenmarket to the new site. The cost of their law suit gave rise to higher prices for slaughtering.[18] However, the council did allow them 1,000 merks compensation when the move took place.[19] The replacement on the west side of the Greenmarket was itself removed when Whitehall Crescent was planned.[20]

Though the Fleshers paid an annual rent to the town for the shambles, as well as a quantity of neat's tongues to the town clerk until well into the eighteenth century, the realisation that they were not in fact in total control of such a vital part of their trade after centuries of apparent independence came as quite a shock to the Trade. To obtain that control and be indeed 'masters of the shambles' seems to have become something of an obsession with at least some members of the incorporation. The results were unfortunate.

During the dispute they began the search for a site for a shambles that would be truly their own. Their first attempt to obtain a property, in the Seagate, was abortive.[21] Relations with the town did not improve and the Trade was given notice to remove from the Greenmarket in 1821. That crisis passed when an increased rent of £100 was agreed. Rents from the several slaughter houses within the shambles, some rented out to one butcher, some to groups, made up £71.14s.0d. of this sum and the Trade's funds had to be called on to make up the balance.[22]

A few years later, in 1826, a 'ruinous tenement' was bought lying between the Overgate and the Ward burn but it was quickly sold when the Trade realised it was unsuitable for their purpose.[23] The same year there was once again disagreement between town and Trade about rent[24] and in March 1828 we find the Fleshers once again actively looking for a new place. They declared that it seemed unlikely that they would be allowed to keep on the current lease.[25]

Following that decision the next few months saw the Fleshers make a series of decisions which were to prove disastrous for their finances for decades. They bought property on the west side of Long Wynd for £300, and after employing James Black as their architect, chose one of his plans and asked for sealed estimates. Fortunately, on this occasion they did not enter into contracts for the new shambles in case neighbours objected to the proposal. As they knew that smithies, steam engines, soap, candle and gas works were already forbidden on the ground concerned, they might have realised that it was unlikely that the nearby proprietors would countenance the practice of their trade there. It could be equally malodorous and on occasion noisy.[26]

Objections were indeed lodged by their prospective neighbours and at the same time, the town clerk reminded them that dues were liable on all animals killed in the town whether in the public shambles or anywhere else. He pointed out that though these dues had not been levied for a long period because of the rent paid to the town by the Trade, the right to them had not been lost. He also made the veiled threat that a further loss of income would result from the disposal of dung, as only that in the public shambles did not automatically belong to the police commissioners. Needless to say the

Trade retorted that they did not accept such claims and that if the town council exacted dues it would then be up to the burgh to provide a slaughterhouse; they understood from the draft of the bill for improving the town that the present one was up for sale.[27]

This crisis passed when the council declared they did not mean to alter the site and were prepared to renew the lease, but the threat unsettled the Fleshers. In 1834 they offered to give up the fleshmarket to the town but as they wanted to keep the slaughterhouses, this offer was refused.[28] The next year they bought property in East Chapelshade, formerly the Dundee Soap Work Company, at the time an engineering works. Slaughterhouses were built with two flats planned above them but once again, neighbouring proprietors objected on two grounds. One was that the 'effluvia rising from carcases and remains of slaughtered animals' would make life there intolerable for human beings, and the other was that access was unsuitable, being only by narrow lanes. The Trade replied that the alleged nuisance was 'altogether visionary', they operated under police regulations and in any case, there were other works there, including a tannery.[29] They had a point, as tanneries ranked high in noisomeness!

Disregarding such obstacles to their plans, the Trade had slaughterhouses built on the site, let the old fleshmarket to a coal merchant and on 17 April decided to enter the new premises to pre-empt the objectors, as they heard that an interdict was being sought. They even allocated slaughterhouses to members and advertised the prospective dung for sale. All this effort was to no avail. On 13 June 1837 the minutes record that they were faced with an interdict preventing killing at the new shambles until all parties involved in the dispute were heard, and in September the sheriff gave his verdict against them. Even worse, they had to pay the pursuers' expenses.[30]

Financially this episode embroiled them in debts which were not cleared for forty years. The Trade's funds were heavily embarrassed from then on. Money had been borrowed to buy the Chapelshade site for £600 and they spent at least £1,500 on building there.[31] Whenever it became clear that it could never become their new shambles they tried in vain to sell the property, despite its advantages as the Trade advertised them: a plentiful water supply and freedom from burgh taxes as the property was situated outside the boundaries of the Royal Burgh. Though warehouses, heckling houses and dwelling houses there brought in some rent, their funds were exhausted when they paid creditors 8s. in the £ in January 1839.[32] It was in fact 1849 before Henry Henderson, a leather merchant renting a tallow house on the premises, relieved them of this financial millstone.[33] The asking price in 1840 had been £2,300 but Henderson paid only £1,200 plus the conveyancing fees.

Considering the financial circumstances it is astonishing to find that only six months after partly clearing their debts in 1839 the Trade once again embarked on acquiring their own shambles.[34] This time Dudhope Nursery, Douglas Street, was the chosen site. In September 1839 the deacon and boxmaster were authorised to borrow money both to build slaughterhouses there and to repay debts due on the Chapelshade site. As well as building slaughterhouses, it was found necessary to buy a neighbouring house for the watchman for £4 and to open up access roads and macadamise them. The contractor engaged to remove rubbish from the Dudhope site complained the roads were so bad, he could not fulfil his bargain and wanted more money.[35] The Dundee Union Bank advanced a further £1,000 and the Trade duly took possession.

Their records thereafter indicate that most of the Fleshers' corporate energy was used in trying to keep some sort of solvency. They moved their debt from one creditor to another, as they found some individual or bank prepared to accept their security. Most who did must have regretted doing so. In 1845[36] servicing debts of over £3,000 absorbed most of an income of £324 which arose from rents at the Chapelshade property of £103; £153 for dung; £50 from the shambles; and non-existent church seat-rents after the 1841 fire.

Two banks, Dundee Union and the Eastern Bank of Scotland were among their creditors, but £1,200 was still due to the seller of Chapelshade. The Fleshers proposed moving the bank debts to the Western Bank of Scotland, something the Dundee Union Bank refused to propose on their behalf. The Western did in fact eventually accept their security for some of their debts and in the 1850s was pressing for repayment.[37] The shambles manure helped cover this debt, the money obtained from the lessee being paid at once into the Western.

Some of the members showed an incredible lack of realism about the Trade's finances. At one point, when one creditor was owed £400 with no prospects of being repaid in the foreseeable future, it was moved – and carried by the eight members present – that all arrears of rent due by members for the slaughterhouses should be 'departed from'. It is hardly surprising that the deacon and boxmaster, the officials who had to deal continually with the Trade's intractable financial problems, left the meeting, the deacon officially dissenting from the motion. Fortunately, more responsible counsels prevailed and a few weeks later this motion was rescinded.[38]

Three years later, however, the officials were once again faced with a resolution that they considered invalid and illegal – that members should be charged no rents at all. This suggestion may of course have been in anticipation of the loss of their privileges, but that subject was not mentioned in that context or indeed anywhere else in the surviving records.[39] Such an attitude must have been particularly galling to the boxmaster. In 1850 William Gibb who was serving at the time had to report that he had no funds at all to pay even poor rates. He offered to settle these accounts himself if he could collect the dues for slaughtering.[40]

What was perhaps the most unfortunate part of the financial imbroglio was that he was not the only individual member whose personal finances became involved. Several gave their personal guarantees of security, first to Captain Scott, the seller of Chapelshade, and then to Dundee Union Bank[41] for the new shambles. A substantial part of the money spent by the Trade came from individual members, who must have felt great loyalty towards their association. Some of them never saw their money again. Their families were gradually recompensed, though not for the full amount if all the interest they should have received had been included.[42]

It may have been the absorption with the problem of their debts which explains the silence of the records on the important subject of proposed legislation abolishing burgh and craft privileges and liberties. Neither before, during or after its passage through parliament was any direct mention made in the remaining minute books of the bill or the eventual act which was so crucial to the very existence of craftsmen's monopolies. Indeed, few public issues merited any mention in their existing records. Small contributions were made during the 1780s to the movement for reform but thereafter it is November 1868 before there is any real attention to outside events, when the Water Bill and a report on the extension to the harbour were discussed.[43]

On the other hand throughout the 1840s and indeed as late as March 1846 the unfree who slaughtered bestial or traded as butchers within the burgh were still being faced with lawsuits. The suggestion was even made in December 1844 that a superintendent of the police should be expected to try to stop the killing of beasts outside the slaughterhouses. One imagines such action would not have received a sympathetic response. Perhaps this is another example of the lack of realism about their financial situation which was so surprising in the attitude of such practical men. Whatever the cause the existing records give no clue to their reactions to their changed legal situation.

The second half of the nineteenth century was to see great changes in attitudes to hygiene and control of public utilities. In 1851 the Trade had to have their slaughterhouse registered in term of a General Police Act adopted by Dundee.[44] The town's regulations in 1854 insisted on flagstone floors, a good water supply, proper ventilation, biannual washing of the walls with quick lime, and the removal of dung, skins and tallow every twenty-four hours.[45] All this activity involved expense for the Trade. When the surrounding springs dried up after the Lochee road was drained, water had to be brought in from Monikie by the Dundee Water company at the cost of £5.5s.0d. per annum.[46] In 1869 the tenants of the slaughterhouses demanded that gas lighting should be installed.[47]

The Trade had some difficulty finding good watchmen. For 12s. per week and a house, the watchman had to keep the shambles clean and orderly and report to the deacon when he thought animals were diseased. Until 1862 when a special appointment was made for the purpose, he also had to collect the dues on animals killed.[48] Because of the amount of money involved in collecting these dues, as long as it was the watchman's responsibility, he had to have cautioners (guarantors). It was clearly an onerous post in which it was difficult to satisfy his employers and there were regular dismissals because of the Trade's dissatisfaction with the way in which watchmen carried out their duties.

The Flesher Trade finally lost its position as 'masters' of the shambles in 1877. The Police Commission wanted to take control and the Trade was eventually deprived of use of the slaughterhouse, receiving £500 in compensation.[49] The buildings and site were sold for £1,000 to Henry Henderson and Son, who had a tan works next door to it. Like the Chapelshade site this price was much reduced from what the Trade first asked.[50] Some of the money was used to clear all their existing debts and the remainder was divided among members.

The Trade, or at least some members, always maintained an elitist and fairly arbitrary stance towards new would-be entrants, quite often refusing admittance to applicants without reasons being given. One wonders why anyone wanted to join a body in such perilous financial state but even more why the Trade would not have welcomed extra members with open arms to help their funds and share the burden of debt. In April 1869, with only six members present, it was resolved that only sons of freemasters of the incorporation should be allowed to join. A few days later a larger number cancelled this motion, probably wisely if the Trade was to survive with a viable membership. In the next hundred years far more unfree joined than sons of freemen. In 1872 the Trade refused to consider allowing their clerk to join, which was very unusual among the Dundee Trades.[51]

Applicants were still expected to perform a test showing their skills in the 1870s and two who failed the first time were refused another attempt. The third on this occasion, whose skills were not in question, was still refused entry until a report on his birth was obtained from Melbourne. There was suspicion that he was only the stepson of his pretended freemaster father![52] Once the shambles was sold the Trade agreed that new members would be admitted only on condition that they concurred with all the incorporation's transactions carried out before their entry. This was decided just before the division of their surplus funds among existing members after the sale of the shambles.[53]

When the new Lockit Book opened perforce on 12 April 1870, two entrants paid their dues. One was unfree, William Wilkie, paying £52.10s. and one free, Robert Kerr Junior, who had to find only £2.10s. Fourteen members attended on this occasion and in September 1871 sixteen elected a new deacon. It was 1892 before more names are entered in the Lockit Book but 39 joined in that decade. There was another hiatus between 1903 and 1916 but since then there has been a small but steady stream of entrants.

The Flesher Trade kept its direct interest in its own craft in a very active way rather longer than others. The ownership and control of the main shambles in the town must undoubtedly have contributed to this interest. The Trade today tends to admit only men whose work has some connection with the meat trade, but there have been exceptions. In 1927 there was a very mixed bag including a banker's agent, a coal merchant and a publican. A wine merchant and a grain merchant became freemasters in 1925 and 1933 and successive ministers of St Andrew's kirk are usually entered as freemasters. There are currently over 80 members[54] which would seem an adequate number to ensure the survival of this ancient Dundee institution, whose trade was and is so vital to the welfare of Dundonians.

NOTES

[1] See Chapter 1, The Trades' Records. Fortunately three volumes, the first dating from 1714, had not been in the desk that was stolen. They provide financial and other information. Mr A.N. Fenton, clerk to the Trade, kindly allowed me access to the records in his possession which refer to the period before the Lockit Book disappeared. (FMB, 1, 2, 3)

[2] NT5.2.1.

[3] Grant, 1930, 135, 136.

[4] Torrie, 1990, 85, 86; Whatley, 1993, 39–41.

[5] Maxwell, 1891, 228.

[6] DDL. F.H.3.

[7] A.C. Lamb, *Dundee, its Quaint and Historic Buildings* (Dundee, 1895), xii. Hereafter Lamb, 1895; Millar, 1925, 176–177.

[8] Maxwell, 1884, 53–54.

[9] Maxwell, 1891, 228.

[10] FB1, 13.11.1784.

[11] FMB3, 30.4.1846.

[12] Ibid., 9.9.1845.

[13] Ibid., 6.3.1845; 13.3.1845.

[14] Ibid., 7.3.1862.

[15] FB1, 1714.

[16] FB1, 1764–65.

[17] Lamb, 1895.

[18] FB1, 13.6.1776.

[19] Ibid., 1775–76 accounts.

[20] Millar, 1925, 176–7.

[21] FB1, 14.8.1776.

[22] FMB2, 2, 6.11.1821; 21.11.1821. All references, 22–35 come from FMB2. Only dates will be cited.

[23] 18.1.1826.

[24] 17.7.1826.

[25] 20.3.1828.

[26] 20.3.1828; 17.9.1828.

[27] 30.9.1828.

[28] 14.12.1834.

[29] 11.8.1835.

[30] 17.4.1837; 15.5.1837; 1.6.1837; 13.6.1837; 26.9.1837.

[31] 4.2.1840.

[32] 24.1.1839.

[33] FMB3, 14, 18.6.1849; 11.11.1849.

[34] FMB2, 17.6.1839.

[35] Ibid., 4.2.1840.

[36] FMB3, 9.9.1845. Dates only, 36–40, as all cited are from FMB3.

[37] 9.7.1858.

[38] 22.9.1842.

[39] 15.12.1845.

[40] 16.5.1851.

[41] FMB2, 25.12.1839.

[42] FMB3, *passim*. Dates only, 42–53, as all are from FMB3.

[43] 2.11.1968.

[44] 3.4.1851.

[45] 11.4.1854.

[46] 26.9.1861; 18.10.1861.

[47] 1.12.1869.

[48] 4.12.1862.

[49] 12.2.1877.

[50] 6.7.1877.

[51] 15.3.1872.

[52] 30.3.1876.

[53] 28.8.1877.

[54] Information from Mr A.N. Fenton.

CHAPTER 10

The Hammermen Trade

The earliest entry in the Hammermen Trade's Lockit Book, dated 26 December 1587, states that it is the book of the 'halmermen' of Dundee and contained within it the names of freemen, entries of apprentices and the various statutes made for the welfare of the craft at that time, when Patrick Ramsay was deacon.[1] The opening of this book was not of course the first act of the incorporation of Hammermen. Some of the statutes entered at this date were undoubtedly adjustments and alterations of previous practices of the Trade.

The Hammermen Trade ranks seventh among the Nine. Its Seal of Cause is lost, but the Nine Trade's Inventory of Charters[2] includes what purports to be a copy giving the date of its being granted as 21 September 1525, during the deaconship of Alexander Moir. The Hammermen undertook to provide sustentation for a chaplain to 'sang and say God save us' before an altar to St Eloy, their patron saint, at the northmost part of the north aisle in the town kirk, which they would maintain. The chaplain was to carry out his duties just as the chaplains of the 'lave (rest) of the crafts of the burgh does'.

Though this may be the only evidence available concerning the date of the formation of an incorporation of hammermen, we can find some proof of its being in operation in the years between then and 1587. Two cutlers were before the burgh court because they had 'invaded' their deacon, Silvester Ramsay with a drawn whinger (a dagger or small sword often attached to a man's belt). As Silvester was the father of Patrick, the deacon in 1587, he presumably served before that date.[3]

Long before 1525 hammermen of all kinds were working in the burgh. A local armourer, Wat Moncur, frequently supplied James IV with specially made suits of armour.[4] Another Moncur, John, was working in Dundee in the 1440s and 1450s.[5] Swords were commonly owned and later in 1556 we have the name of one swordmaker, George Lovell, working in the burgh; blades he had made for a customer were arrested to pay for the craftsman's debts.[6] The first list of 35 master hammermen in their Lockit Book includes seven who made parts of swords. In a town as important as Dundee where gold and silver ornaments and belts were frequently worn, owned and fought over, and silver spoons were used as currency, gold and silversmiths must have set up their booths.[7]

Unfortunately, despite the eminence of the Trade in the past, the Lockit Book is now the only historic document which remains in the clerk's care. Originally, a statement of what the book was to contain was followed by a list of all the hammermen in Dundee and next by the rules of the Trade as laid down in 1758. This was how Warden found it,[8] but since then the book has been rebound – very beautifully, it should be said – and as usual in such circumstances, the entries are now out of order.

Today we find two blank pages after that first entry, followed by the entrant's oaths written in a later hand. Thereafter various documents, random in date and subject, have been inserted into the book by modern methods of conservation, which should preserve them. The first we find is a servant's contract of 1617 by which Andrew Young, changing masters from father to son, was to receive a set of clothes, a knife and fork and a pair of shoes yearly for three years. A 1651 disagreement about an account sent by Richard Air, a saddler, comes next, then a 1602 licence to a hammerman from Strathdichty, David Thane. He was to be allowed to work in Dundee paying his weekly penny to the Trade, but which particular branch of the craft he practised was not specified.

The most interesting document in the general context of Dundee is that recording the expulsion of Alexander Guthrie from the incorporation for striking the deacon and 'other causes not decent to publish'. In the relevant entry in the Lockit Book there was less reticence about his misdeeds. He had been entered as a saddler in April 1645 and beside this entry the reason for his expulsion is given, where of course it would be expected to be kept secret from contemporaries outside the Trade. Guthrie had been disobedient to the deacon and had been guilty of 'filthie carriage to his brethren by lying daily to the English commander'. The date of the expulsion is not recorded but as David Nicoll was deacon, his misdemeanours must have occurred or at least been discovered in 1653–54.

Though Guthrie's expulsion might indicate that the Hammermen were moved by anti-English feeling at this time, there must be some doubt about this suggestion when we find that they admitted two Englishmen to their ranks about the same time. In 1649, Richard Air, the man whose account was queried in 1651, was entered and in October 1654, Henry Morley, an Englishman, handed in his essay and was accepted as freemaster. What does seem to emerge is that the English forces had some support in Dundee, despite the horrors of Monck's sack of the burgh, though Guthrie may have been a solitary example. On 19 November 1660, a saddler, John Barnett, another Englishman, was entered twice, the first time with some restrictions on his privileges which were almost immediately crossed out.

It must have been quite difficult for the hammermen to get together as a society. All who worked mainly with a hammer and metal were eligible for membership and as a result, over the centuries twenty or more crafts figure in their records. On occasion, some of these crafts are amalgamated. When George Dempster of Dunnichen became a freemaster on 10 June 1761, 'goldsmith and jewler', 'clocksmith and watchmaker', 'coppersmith and white ironsmith' were clearly not considered totally separate activities but the entry for George Duncan, MP on 30 November 1842 does list them separately. Not all who qualified as knocksmiths, for instance, were also given credit as watchmakers. The others mentioned in the eighteenth and nineteenth centuries include blacksmith, gunsmith, sword slipper, cutler, locksmith, farrier, saddler, lorimer, brassfounder, plumber, pewterer, guardmaker and potter. Two ancient trades which do not appear in later times are armourer and bucklemaker. Alexander Smith was the last armourer to join in November 1684.

One group of hammermen obtained permission from the town council and the deacons to separate themselves from the incorporation. The goldsmiths had fallen out with their Trade for reasons now unknown and it was apparently impossible to resolve the quarrel. On 26 October 1602 the provost, bailies, council *and* the deacons of craft 'dissolvit and separated' the goldsmiths from the society and fellowship of the brethren of the Hammermen Craft. They were to be exempt from the jurisdiction of the deacon and from paying the weekly penny or any other contributions imposed. The proviso was made, however, that goldsmiths were not to elect a deacon without the consent of the town council.[9] All goldsmiths did not stay aloof from the Hammermen Trade despite this arrangement. On 26 August 1614 Thomas Cyd gave in his essay and became a freemaster hammerman. His name does not appear in the index to the burgess Lockit Book kept in Dundee Public Library, but on the other hand, Patrick Gardyne and Thomas Houre, registered in 1624 and 1651 respectively as *aurifaber*, goldsmith, (as many trades were given in Latin in that volume) do not seem to have entered the Trade. The burgess list indicates that goldsmiths were thin on the ground in the burgh during the seventeenth century, even before Monck's onslaught.[10]

Gold and silver work came under the same label. Dundee goldsmiths were few but many Dundee silversmiths made admirable work, without necessarily joining the Hammermen Craft. For instance the name of William Scott who made the communion plate for St Andrew's, the Trades' Kirk, does not seem to be entered in the Lockit Book. Craftsmen who moved into the burgh from other places might have been more inclined to secure their position at least before the loss of burgh and craft privileges; there are entries of goldsmiths among the many hammermen of all persuasions who came to make their living in Dundee in the eighteenth and nineteenth centuries. Though the burgh lost its right to a separate hallmark in 1836 when Parliament then enacted that all Scottish silver and gold must be sent to Edinburgh to be tested, some silversmiths retained the distinctive Dundee pot of lilies in their personal marks.[11]

Usually, but not invariably, a man's particular trade was recorded when he became a freemaster. The Trade tried to keep its various skills in separate branches, on the grounds that they did not wish to be known as jacks of all trades and masters of none. The first statutes recorded in the Lockit Book in 1587 indicate that masters in some branches had been usurping the work of others. The Trade at this point forbade masters to employ servants to 'forge or mak ony kynd of wark' in which the master himself was not experienced or could not finish. Goldsmiths were to confine themselves to making articles of gold and silver, cutlers to knives, gunmakers to pistols, sword slippers to scabards and finishing off cuirasses and armour. Lorimers could make only stirrups, bits and spurs, while saddlers dealt with saddles and harnesses. Pots and pans were to come from the potter, and stoups (drinking vessels), plates and trenchers from the pewterer.

Trespassing on other men's specialities had not been stopped by the 1587 statutes, however, and on 8 April 1663 the Trade repeated the rule that a member should practise only that branch in which he had given his essay and 'masterstick'. It was almost 300 years before the Hammermen relaxed their attitude on such behaviour. The last master whose employment was restricted was William Whyte, a Lochee engineer. He entered the Trade on 9 October 1911 and it was laid down that he could do the work of an engineer 'allenarly' (only). There were no further names entered in the Lockit Book until 1921 when Christopher Bisset was entered with no professional qualifications mentioned, and James Whyte was admitted engineer on 25 September 1930 as an engineer with no restrictions on his work.

Since that date, the Lockit Book has not always recorded a master's qualifications but the traditions of the Trade are maintained. On 6 December 1955 some new rules made by the general meeting included one that restricted membership to men engaged in a trade in which working with metal and the use of a hammer played an important part. However, masters' sons and sons-in-law could be admitted whatever their occupation. All had to have their homes or business within the city of Dundee or within ten miles from its boundaries.

A few masters throughout the centuries qualified in several crafts. John Walls, for instance was entered as both a cutler and a clocksmith on 15 December 1715. On 8 June 1691 Andrew Baisler was apparently qualified to act as blacksmith and goldsmith. If they did indeed serve apprenticeships in both their crafts, they were not young when finally becoming freemasters for hammermen were bound to serve at least five years plus one for meat and fee. On several occasions in the mid-seventeenth century, seven, eight and nine years training were specified when the apprentice was entered in the book. One craftsman, Alexander Smith, was first entered as master clockmaker and gunsmith in August 1718. He was the son of George Smith, also a joint master in both trades. In 1727, when he was deacon, another master stood in for him when he was admitted as a goldsmith. There were some incongruous occupations. William Douglas, a wigmaker, was recognised as a master goldsmith on 4 June 1719, the same day that a merchant joined as a blacksmith. Perhaps they were honorary members but there is no clue in the Lockit Book, except that both were entered on the same day.

The preponderance of craftsmen connected with weaponmaking is significant in the earlier records, reflecting society of the time just as the occupations of entrants in the nineteenth century demonstrated Dundee's industrial development. The first list of 35 included eight gunmakers, five sword slippers making sword blades, a gairdmaker who produced the hilt, three locksmiths who would make the locks for guns as well as the more pacific domestic locks, and three cutlers whose 'whingers' appear in so many Dundee court cases. In the middle years of the nineteenth century the Trade accommodated some new occupations such as machinemaker by entering masters as practitioners of older crafts such as blacksmith.[12] An ironmonger, Alexander Lawson, was described as a tinsmith.[13] On the other hand in the 1790s a coach, cart and ploughmaker and a machinemaker were admitted under their professed trades.[14]

One branch of the Hammermen Trade brought fame to the town in the late sixteenth and early seventeenth centuries. Dundee guns were famous all over Europe. Scottish pistols of this period were generally much admired, though perhaps more as badges of rank and as special official gifts than as weapons of war. It has been suggested that mercenaries on their way to join European armies would have bought them in Dundee before

151

embarking.[15] David Wedderburne, the merchant whose *Compt Buik* tells us so much about Dundee merchandise, exported a few, some to Spain.[16]

Dundee seems to have been the chief centre of the craft of gunmaking in Scotland. The families of Ramsays and Alisons were prominent in the local Trade, but an eminent craftsman of the time engraved his initials I.L. on at least some of the lock plates he made and may have been James Low, the locksmith whose name appears in the first list in the Hammermen's Lockit Book.[17] A high proportion of the members recorded between 1587 and 1650 were gunmakers. In the 1630s several were entered as dagmakers, a dag being a heavy pistol, a term more often used in Glasgow than in Dundee. Thereafter the numbers decreased and the industry became less important in the burgh. As usual, Monck's sacking has been blamed[18] but about 1650 fashions in decorating the butts changed as did lock patterns; perhaps the Dundee gunmakers did not adapt and thereby lost their pre-eminence.

The craft did not die out completely and there were still some gunsmiths working or at least joining the Trade in the eighteenth century. David MacKenzie became a gunsmith in 1707, then in 1722 was admitted as a sword slipper as well. MacKenzie's son, James, also was 'received as such', both gunmaker and swordslipper in January 1728, and a son of David's widow, John Jameson, also joined as a gunsmith in 1733. The next practitioner entered was David MacKenzie, son of James, a gunsmith in Brechin, admitted in January 1751. He may have been a grandson of the first David, but no suggestion is made that his father was a Dundee master. The last gunsmith entered was John Hight or Flight in 1764.

Unfortunately little is known about methods or even about the styles made in the burgh or in Scotland in earlier times. No description of essays by gunmakers is given in the Lockit Book – indeed only one test is detailed, that of a blacksmith.[19] The Dundee craftsmen made guns of 'fishtail' and 'lemon butt' design and two beautiful examples can now be seen in the National Museums of Scotland, Queen Street, Edinburgh but whether other types were made is not known. Hammermen began to find other ways of making a living as weapons like guns and swords were less often made in the burgh. New industries provided opportunities for a different type of craftsmanship and as we have seen the Trade began to find ways of accommodating these new skills.

Like all the trade incorporations, the Hammermen tried to maintain standards and their monopolistic privileges. Keeping the work of the unfree out of the burgh on the grounds that it was not up to standard was one of their gambits. On 5 December 1696 the Trade laid down the rule that the unfree must sell their wares on market days only, where they would be laid out for inspection like those of the freemen. Any offending would have their goods seized and sold for the poor. Ninety years previously, on 14 July 1606, the Trade had unanimously agreed that no alien servants (i.e. men from outside Dundee) were to be allowed to become masters. At the same time, the husbands of daughters of freemen could no longer automatically expect to become members on the same conditions as their brothers-in-law. This would help to restrict the numbers.

Other privileges which the Trade kept for itself as a community included sharpening knives and shears for other artisans, particularly waulkers. The deacon had to provide and maintain a grindstone for the purpose so that the resulting income went to the Trade's box and not to individual members, all of whom were likely to own their own.[20] The deacon alone was also enjoined to buy the special coal, smiddy coal, needed for hammermen's forges as it arrived at the port, and this fuel had to be specially and separately weighed and delivered so that the poor fund received its just dues as each master paid for his allocation.

Another restriction has a phrase in it which is incomprehensible today. In November 1657 craftsmen were forbidden to make steel of iron for merchants by 'cleaming heid gales'. Even the editors of the *Dictionary of the Older Scottish Tongue* have been unable to find the meaning of this phrase.[21] It is not clear whether the iron treated belonged to the merchant or the hammerman.

The records contain one very interesting comment on an economic trend which is only too familiar to the twentieth century. Inflation was a familiar phenomenon to some of our forefathers and on 9 December 1622 it was decided to double the weekly payments due from master and servant from one penny Scots for masters and a halfpenny for servants. These dues had been fixed 'ane long time since', when they claimed the one penny was of greater value and could purchase more than two could currently.

Like all the local Trades the Hammermen were affected by general economic conditions. At their meeting in the 'burial place of Dundie' on 26 October 1698, during 'King William's ill years' they recorded that they had been compelled to contract debts 'through severall reasons known to themselves'. The increase in the needs of the poor was the main reason. They increased the quarterly accounts to 3s.4d. Each Head Court day 13s.4d. was to be paid to the deacon. Like other Trades in similar circumstances they cancelled the 'banket' given by masters and apprentices on the occasion of their entry and imposed an extra fee of £8 on 'alien' masters, the unfree, instead of the dinner, and £5 on freemasters' sons plus £5 for the quart of wine they usually provided and £12 booking money. Free apprentices were to pay £20 without a banquet. Finally the deacon was to stop all banquets, feasts and unnecessary drinking paid out of the Trade's funds. The Hammermen, it should be remembered, were not alone in carousing on the profits of the poor box!

The following year, on 31 August 1699, the Trade tapped their journeymen too for additional funds. It was alleged that the welfare of the Trade was being damaged by their leaving masters to whom they had engaged themselves. They were in future to pay 16s. each time they moved, as well as paying £1.10s. to the Trade for their booking, while masters were to pay 10s., if a servant remained with them for one year.

In January 1728 during another bad period the 'inconsiderable' booking money was once again augmented for the benefit of the poor fund. Unfree were to pay 100 merks for their freedom, £60 Scots for booking and to serve a year as officer. Free apprentices were to pay at least £60 Scots for their booking but this was 'without prejudice' to freemen's sons. They were not to be so penalised. The deacon in 1733, George Miller, thought that there was no act by which the dues were clearly stated and insisted on having this situation remedied. The sons and sons-in-law of freemasters were to pay £12 Scots in total. The unfree on the other hand paid £3 at their first court, when applying for entry, 100 merks for their freedom, £2 for the opening of the Lockit Book, £12 booking money, 5 merks to the General Fund of the Nine Trades, £12 officer's fees and the obligation to serve as officer and £4 for benefit of the Trade's seats in the church and the mortcloth.

The difference is startling and might reflect the favourable position of the Hammermen in attracting new members until the mid-nineteenth century. The Trade has had a regular flow of entrants throughout its history until the abolition of all trade privileges in 1846. Between 1600 and 1699 over 160 men joined as masters, 150 by 1799 and the flow did not dry up until 1847, as just over 100 joined between 1800 and that date. There was then a gap until 1862 and by 1874 there were eleven new hammermen. What happened next is impossible to say with only the Lockit Book available but the only entries are of examination by the General Fund Court until August 1903 when John Whytock became a freemaster jeweller, not at liberty to practise any other branch of the Hammermen's trades. He was the son of the deacon, also John, who had joined the Trade in September 1869.

There were only four more entries of members from then until 1931 when there seems to have been a drive to increase numbers – five in 1931, one in 1934 and then a comparative flood in 1936 and 1938 when eleven in all joined with two more in the next two years. In 1955 when a new set of rules were drawn up including an oath promising still to 'obtemper and fulfill' the rules, 28 members signed plus the deacon, boxmaster and clerk. The Trade has enrolled almost 150 members since then.

The regularity with which the Trade has seen its numbers grow must surely reflect the extremely important part the various crafts of the Dundee Hammermen have played in Dundee's economic growth. The Trade can probably claim to have been the most famous of the Nine Trades in earlier centuries, largely through the skill of their gunsmiths. Later the traditional skills in working metal must have helped industrial development when metal was increasingly used in factory machinery while the artistry of eighteenth and nineteenth century silversmiths is highly respected. It is quite an achievement for a comparatively small group of Dundonians.

NOTES

[1] The Hammerman Trade's Lockit Book (HMLB) is in the care of the clerk of the Trade, Mr G.F. Ritchie. When it is clear that the Lockit Book is the source of material, no reference is given, except to specify dates not given in the text.

[2] NT5.2.1.

[3] Maxwell, 1891, 355.

[4] Lamb, 1895, ii.

[5] David Caldwell, *The Scottish Armoury* (Edinburgh, 1979), 14.

[6] Maxwell, 1891, 265.

[7] Maxwell, 1891, 253–5.

[8] Warden, 1872, 472.

[9] Maxwell, 1884, 302–303.

[10] DDL. F.H.3; HMLB.

[11] 6 & 7 W.IV c.69; Abertay Historical Society Lecture by W. Guthrie, 8.12.1993.

[12] HMLB, 11.8.1836.

[13] HMLB, 9.9.1833.

[14] HMLB, 23.12.1791; 20.11.1792.

[15] Geoffrey Boothroyd, 'Birth of the Scottish Pistol' in David H. Caldwell, *Scottish Weapons and Fortifications, 1100–1800* (1981), 335. Hereafter Boothroyd, 1981.

[16] Millar (ed.), *The Compt Buik of David Wedderburne* (Edinburgh, 1898), 113.

[17] Boothroyd, 1981, 333, 335.

[18] Boothroyd, 1981, 337.

[19] HMLB, 11.1.1745.

[20] HMLB, 2.9.1662.

[21] Letter from Harry D. Watson, Senior Editor of *The Dictionary of the Older Scottish Tongue*, 15.4.1994.

6. THE HOWFF

(The *Courier*, Dundee)

CHAPTER 11

The Weaver Trade – The Brabiners

Considering the importance of textiles in the Dundee economy during the fifteenth century when the Scottish trades began to seek status as incorporations, it is surprising that the Weavers did not stand higher in precedence there. Ranked eighth of the Nine Trades, weavers had a more vital role in the local and national economy than that position might indicate, as did waulkers, the ninth. If we are to believe the satirist, Sir David Lindsay, there was some distrust of clothmakers and this may have had some influence on their position. According to Lindsay:

Find me ane webster that is leal
Or ane waulker that will nocht steal
Their craftiness I ken.[1]

Hector Boece described Dundee in the early sixteenth century as a town where many virtuous people made cloth, but the various acts passed by parliament trying to control the quality of Scottish cloth throw some doubts on the universal virtuousness of weavers. In 1540 it was laid down that webs should be examined and sealed[2] and Dundee appointed a sealmaster some years later. The town council insisted in 1577 that weavers should weave their own marks into all their webs and in 1701 that yarn sold at the market cross must be of sufficient thickness and length.[3]

Clothmaking was subject to close scrutiny by monarch and parliament because of its importance in the export trade. Bakers might have to weigh their loaves and fleshers slaughter their animals at times and places according to town council decrees, but their products were not so carefully controlled by the national government. Dundee bakers did not export their shortbread in medieval and early modern times, but poorly woven cloth, shorter or narrower than agreed standards, and unevenly fulled webs could have a very adverse effect on the reputation of all the Scottish products.

The Dundee Weaver Trade was in trouble in 1667. A merchant in the

157

burgh, David Wemyss, accused them of selling him narrow cloth which transgressed an act of the Scottish parliament of 1661 regulating the breadth of webs of linen cloth.[4] He had had letters of horning sent to them but they managed to have these suspended. Letters of horning were a Scottish legal step which technically outlawed the recipients. Their defence was somewhat ingenuous. Declaring that they were totally opposed to anyone breaking laws, they argued that even if they had done so they were 'exceeding poor persons' who could not in any case pay the fine. They went on to claim that they did not buy or sell yarn; nor did they make any cloth, narrow or broad, for themselves or for the market but only for supplying the inhabitants of Dundee. In other words, as they were not trying to export cloth they did not think the breadth was of importance.

The Weaver Trade's official Seal of Cause is dated 1 April 1512[5] but the Dundee weavers had been working together long before that date. The Trade possess a sasine for a tenement in the Seagate dated 1475 but neither weavers nor their particular saint are mentioned therein.[6] On 24 August 1492 weavers were clearly acting in a corporate fashion when their deacon, James Guild, and masters of the Trade, then calling itself the brabners (*sic*) appeared before the town council. They wanted permission to set up an altar in the town church in honour of St Severus, their patron saint. It was to be situated on the north side of the choir beside that recently founded in honour of Magnus the Martyr.[7]. After the altar was founded other property was bought, one land in the Fluckergate in 1511 specifically in the name of St Severus, that is for the purpose of keeping the altar in good condition.

In the tolbooth in 1512 the council and bailies confirmed this arrangement, at the same time recognising various enactments already made by the Trade including the weavers' right to elect a deacon. The rules made were similar to those of all the other incorporated Trades: insistence on masters becoming burgesses: the length of apprenticeships: orders against the pirating of other weavers' work unless it had sat unfinished for twenty days: and others of the kind.[8] The Seal of Cause was ratified under the common seal on 25 September 1525 and under the Great Seal on 4 March 1530/31, on both occasions at Dundee.[9] In the years between the first proposal to build St Severus' altar and 1512 the Trade had been buying property in various parts of the town, the income from which was to help maintain the altar and its chaplain.[10]

Despite these arrangements the Trade seems to have failed in its commitment to the altar some time after 1512. One of the main reasons seems to have been the lack of security concerning the box in which were kept the funds for the altar and chaplain. Too many weavers had access to it and were borrowing from it, without repaying their debts which amounted to almost £400 Scots. The chaplain, Sir William Boyd, took action. He and the Weaver Trade agreed on arbitrators, who included two priests, eminent locally, Mr James Scrymgeour, chanter of Brechin, Mr John Barr, vicar of Dundee, and several Dundee burgesses. Their decision, in the shape of a decreet arbitral, was recorded on 21 March 1530.[11]

The panel of arbitrators decided that all debts must be paid in two parts, half before the following Whitsunday, the rest eight days before St Severus' day. To avoid misuse of funds in the future, all fees imposed on weavers, apprentices, servants and masters, duly counted with a receipt from the chaplain, were to be put in St Severus' box every Monday. Annual fees were also to be deposited in the box in presence of the chaplain, the deacon, whoever kept the keys of the box – two 'famous men' of the Craft – and all the rest of the masters of the Craft. Somewhat confusingly the deacon was ordered to keep the kist while at the same time it was to be put 'in ane famous manis house'. Fines were laid down for those who did not pay, while those who could not were to be banished from the town for a year.

The chaplain for his part was to carry out his religious duties for £6 unless he failed the Craft, in which case a complaint could be made to the arbitrators. He was to employ his brother, Sir David, or some other 'sufficient' man if the need arose. A few days later on 27 March, the ruinous state of the altar was admitted in a renewed agreement to maintain it and the chaplaincy. The deacon, Henry Lyell, and 22 other masters undertook this obligation on behalf of themselves and their successors.[12]

The Weaver Trade's connection with the organisation of religion in the parish continued after the Reformation, as in common with all the other incorporations they owned seats in the kirks that were formed out of the great old kirk. In 1830 their income from their pews in the Old and the South kirks amounted to £17.14s.6d.[13] out of which they had to clean and maintain them and employ a servant to ensure each Sunday that no interlopers tried to sit in them. In 1836 they were faced with a demand from the town council for £200 towards repairs, which some heritors had refused to pay. In the circumstances their decision, after seeing the plans for rebuilding after the great fire of 1841, to renounce all their rights in the two kirks is hardly surprising.[14]

The Weavers have used four Lockit Books during their history, only two of which seem to have had keys.[15] Though the Trade has such a comprehensive archive, dating from the fifteenth century, the first Lockit Book entry is dated 1557. As it seems unlikely that such a careful Trade would have lost what most incorporations considered their most important record, we may legitimately wonder if they did not in fact possess one before that date. If that was so they compensated by using two to record a meeting held in Greyfriars Kirk in November 1557, apparently with officials of the town council in attendance.[16] The meeting enacted that servants could fee themselves only on St Thomas' day, masters and servants being liable to fines if they did not adhere to this rule.

In one of the Lockit Books blank pages follow and then a master's entry of 1667/8 appears.[17] A few pages after the entry of a few more masters between 1668 and 1673 a decision of September 1682 is recorded, that masters must pay the thesaurer for their burgess ticket before being admitted masters. In this Lockit Book we then find masters' entries, one of 1627, and 27 where the dates seem somewhat haphazard, 1631 to 1648. The next entry is dated 22 March 1670, and from then until 1698 masters are entered from both burgh and Hill, followed by free apprentices from 1706 to 1769 with a solitary boy's name appearing in 1791.

The other Lockit Book recording the meeting of 1557 was much more regularly and extensively used until the middle of the eighteenth century.[18] The entries include the names of new masters and apprentices and the rules of the Trade, somewhat haphazardly, as is usual in Lockit Books, even those which have not been rebound. The third book enters masters and apprentices until 1762. Beginning at the back of the book a few seventeenth century statutes of the Trade are recorded, including an undated oath making the usual promises of loyalty to king, country, town council, respect for the deacons' orders and the undertaking to promote concord among the brethren.[19]

The Trade paid £22.8s. Scots for a new book in the 1760s[20] which was handsomely rebound a few years ago, using the original brass hasps and decoration. The first entry is the set of the burgh of Dundee as it stood in 1708. The names of all freemasters alive on 6 June 1761 are then recorded, 119 of them, one having entered the Trade in 1706. The entry of new masters begins with that of three honorary members, George Dempster of Dunnichen, Richard Neilson and Robert Speid in June 1761 and continues until today.

No statutes of the Trade are entered in this Lockit Book but between entries of 1770 and 1771 on p. 22 a poem is glued into the book. The first verse calls down blessings on friends of the Weaver Trade in four lines and underneath two fourteen-line verses are at right angles across the page. The first lauds the art of the weaver, pointing out that it has been essential for rich and poor since the 'great Fall'. The second uses the speed of the shuttle, the cutting of the thread, etc., to draw moral lessons about the shortness of life.

Towards the end of the book an alphabetical list of members was begun but is not complete. A copy of the 1697 constitution of the General Fund court and a record of some other General Fund business and Nine Trade rules are also written in. The Lockit Book was respected but one of the sederunt books gives signs of boredom on the clerk's part, lightened by his skill as an amateur cartoonist. In 1781 on the end paper at the back of the book he portrays Robert Elder, junior, who was later both boxmaster and deacon, and there are other doodles with which he whiled away the time during meetings.[21]

Journeymen figure hardly at all in the Trade's extensive archive, except in rules about servants. No lists of entrants seem to exist either loose or in Lockit Books. As with the Lockit Books one feels that it is possible that for some reason about which we can only surmise, the Trade simply did not enter journeymen separately.

References to the Hill weavers abound throughout the Weavers' records. All the Dundee Trades were very wary of any possible invasion of their privileges by Hill masters, whose proximity made it easy for some workers to sneak themselves or their work into Dundee and pass it off as that of local masters. The Weaver and Tailor Trades, however, seem to be the only incorporations that tried to control this by regulating the place of the Hill men in their societies. The Weavers made more formal arrangements than the Tailors. The more usual practice among the other Dundee Crafts seems to have been simply to warn them off or allow them to work under licence, though again the lack of full records may give a deceptive impression about this matter.

In the last two decades of the sixteenth century it was not only Dundee weavers who were concerned about the amount of cloth that was being woven outside the Royal Burghs and sold inside. From the landward areas, from the suburbs and from less privileged towns without royal charter, webs were finding their way into the burghs. In 1584 Edinburgh town council responded to the pleas of the Weaver and Walker Crafts there by reinforcing their privileges vis-à-vis the unfree.

In 1592 the Dundee town council also sprang to the defence of the local craftsmen when they gave in their plea for help in much the same terms as the Edinburgh craftsmen. They claimed they were 'uterly decayit' by losing work to the unfree, who were of course undercutting them. The council insisted that no townsmen should employ unfree weavers in the Rottenrow (Hill town), in the suburbs or any living half a mile north or south of the burgh. Any discovered doing so would have their goods forfeited.[22] In return the deacons of both Trades promised to make good any skaith (damage) done to customers' webs.

This act of the council strengthened the Dundee Trade in its relations with the Hill men and the result was an extraordinary undertaking by the latter on 28 June 1592. Holding up their right hands the Hill weavers, presumably some of them as well taught and qualified in their craft as the Dundee masters, swore by the Evangelist that they would become apprentices of the Brabiner Craft for five years. After that period they must become burgesses of Dundee before being received by the society. They also agreed to pay the same rates to apprentices and servants as were current in Dundee, for example, 10s. and a pair of shoes.[23] Not that the Hill masters were the only employers who paid wages which were over-generous in the eyes of the Trade. In October 1589 when Thomas Cappine was deacon, this practice was deplored as it was believed it allowed servants to despise masters and change their employment at will. It was decreed that 10s. was the largest bounty that could be given.[24]

The steps taken to try to protect the Dundee weavers' privileges were never wholly effective and had to be renewed in 1594, 1600 and 1636.[25] In the 1680s various weavers admitted that they were working in Dundee though they were not members of the Trade. Though in 1685 several were sent letters of horning, breaches of privilege continued and on 1 August 1691 offenders were summoned to appear before the Lords of Council and Session.[26]

Another method of dealing with transgressors was to arrest them. Town officers had been authorised to 'fortify' the Weaver deacons and masters in seizing webs, yarn or cloth being passed to the unfree or to weavers outside the burgh in 1594.[27] A century later the Dundee craftsmen took even stronger steps and arrested a cotton weaver from Strathmartine, Robert Miller. He was kept in custody until he paid 10 merks for his sins and promised never in the future to work cloth of any description, thick or thin, woollen or linen, for Dundee burgesses.[28]

The increasing use of cotton as the eighteenth century progressed posed another problem for incorporated trades in Scotland. In 1804 a letter from the Lanark Weavers arrived asking for financial help in the case they were bringing against cotton weavers.[29] They believed that the cotton trade had no rights such as were granted by parliament to linen-making in George II's reign. The Dundee Trade did not feel their funds allowed them to contribute but they were optimistic about the outcome. Corresponding with the Perth Weaver Trade on the subject they quoted a case in 1778. Silk manufacturers had lost their claim that the Glasgow Weavers' privileges did not include the monopoly of weaving silk, despite the admission by the Glasgow Trade that none of them could in fact weave that yarn. In light of such contradictions in the position of craftsmen, their eventual loss of privilege is hardly surprising.

One of the greatest difficulties facing almost all free craftsmen was that the inhabitants of Dundee and of other Royal Burghs were not at all averse to using the cheaper labour available outside burgh boundaries. Locally it was known that weavers were coming into the Hill from all quarters as access to the Dundee market was so easy from that area. Though Dundee council officers were authorised to assist the Weaver Trade to confiscate any work done within a two mile limit, the illicit trade continued. In 1600 the Hill weavers undertook to look out for incomers and report them to the deacon but the unfree continued to migrate to the areas round the burgh to work and sell their produce in the burgh.

By 1656, at least some of the Dundee Trade must have decided that some form of united action between the two groups was a more efficient way of controlling the Hill. On 25 June that year it was agreed that two Hill weavers would attend the Trade's council and that all would share in the taxes imposed by Dundee town council.[30] In February 1660 the councils of the Hill and Dundee Trades agreed that all the Hill could demand was that two of their number should be considered free in Dundee.[31]

Despite this somewhat limited agreement, a great deal of co-operation is in evidence in the records, though there are also signs that the relationship was not always an easy one. Apprentices indentured to Hill masters were entered in the Dundee Lockit Book, as were Hill masters from at least 1654, and Hill councillors were present at meetings from the 1670s. On the other hand on 22 March 1670 the Trade rescinded some privileges granted to the Hill weavers by the deacon, James Davie, and some of the Trade's council in January of that year.

Part of the objection to the agreement seems to have been that Davie made some concessions 'without consent of the body of the Trade'. The only record as to what these were does not emerge in the records until November 1682 when problems arose in connection with this incident which will be looked at below. The Hill weavers had managed to persuade the deacon to grant them for a very small sum a bond allowing them their freedom, quite against all the Trade's existing rules. At the time the Trade as a whole expressed disapproval in no uncertain terms as they thought that the agreement gave too much advantage to the Hill men.[32]

The town council also seems to have been worried about the threat to burgesses from outsiders. In response to a petition, in June 1670 Charles II strengthened the privileges of incorporated crafts by allowing the council to prohibit all unfreemen from practising any craft in the suburbs of the town. The penalty was to be forfeiture of their goods.[33]

Some years later in September 1682, the Trade once again seems to have had doubts about its neighbours in the Hill. (It may be noted that this entry in the Lockit Book precedes that of March 1670 by several pages, as do entries regarding masters between 1627 to 1648.) The deacon was given precise instructions to admit no-one as a freemaster before the entrant had made arrangements with the town treasurer about becoming a free burgess. Those who did not comply were debarred from voting for magistrates – 'particularly the weavers in the Hill'.

The distinct impression is gained that these clauses show some un-certainty among the Dundee weavers where their Hill colleagues were concerned. The Trade certainly decreed that no-one living outside the burgh, either in the Hill or in the suburbs, was eligible to be deacon. Any deacon who disregarded these orders was in danger of being 'degraded'. But they confirmed later in the statute that Hill weavers would not be admitted masters, not even for their own lives as 'liferenters', unless they had already become freemen.

Their doubts are perhaps excusible when it appears that the Hill town weavers had not destroyed their copy of the 1670 bond although it had been annulled. A meeting of the whole Craft had been called by the Collector of the Nine Trades, James Lowson, after those displeased with the arrange-ment had appealed to him.[34] However, some time before November 1682 the current deacon, James Hazelles, had got possession of the Hill copy. What happened next is not clear but apparently he gave the document back to the Hill men, who somewhat surprisingly returned it to him. At that point Hazelles declared he would keep it, despite apparently having been attacked physically. He and other masters made a sworn statement before a Notary Public but the matter disappears from the records. The Hill men were not in a strong position.

Once Dundee had purchased the barony of the Hilltown in 1697 the relationship was bound to change and thereafter no anti-Hill rules appear. However, masters were still entered 'to the Hill' as late as 1718 and two Hilltown weavers as such continued to attend meetings of the Dundee Trade's council until well on in the eighteenth century.

Apart from Hill weavers, there were occasionally other entries which were a little out of the ordinary. In 1671 we find the Weavers making an unusual contract with Patrick Cocke who was a weaver, an indweller in

Dundee, but not apparently a member of the Craft. For 'a certain soume', the Weaver Trade gave him the free liberty of working on one loom for his lifetime. He bound himself to work for any free master weaver in Dundee. At the time he was George Ower's servant and perhaps could not afford the full dues, for it is stated in the contract that if he 'seeks the labour of a free master, he shall produce and deliver to the said craft and the thesaurer of the said burgh his receipt or discharge of the libertie of his burgessship'. This seems to be giving him permission to become a master at a later date, but with permission to work only one loom the contract did not enable him either to employ a journeyman or to train an apprentice.[35] A good supply of equipment was needed before a craftsman could exercise these options.

Reeds were part of that essential equipment and reedmakers could be given preferential treatment. In 1642 John Galloway – and his bairns to come efter him – was allowed to set up two looms as long as the Trade was provided with all types of reed they required at set prices, 2d. and 8d. for the carriage of his stuff and 2d. per hundred of 'boges'.[36]

Quite apart from changing industrial practices the Weavers like all incorporated Trades in the growing towns faced the problem of what to do about unfree workers who practised their craft almost with impunity within the old burgh bounds. The Weavers also had to deal with reluctant payers of quarterly accounts within their ranks. By 1825 they were prepared to consider abandoning regular payments and in 1832 a General Meeting of the Trade carried a motion to that effect, but made it clear that those who had stopped contributing before that date had no claim on the funds.[37] At that point entry dues were also fixed at £13 for the unfree, £8 for sons-in-law and £5 for freemasters' sons. No entrant was to be over 40 years old and sons-in-law must be under 30, though in 1835 this limit was raised to 40. Older entrants were more likely to make earlier demands on the poor box and most Trades imposed age limits on entrants at one time or another.[38]

The Trade's records make little comment on the approaching loss of privilege which took place in 1846. This has been attributed to the prosperity among weavers at the time, but it might also have been due to the decreasing numbers joining the incorporation. In 1836 they decided to appoint a committee to ascertain the value of the incorporation's property as they remarked that 'an Act of Parliament proposed annihilating corporations.'[39] They had been investing in property in the town as recently as 1824 as bank interest rates were so low. They had then bought Donaldson's Croft in Bucklemaker Wynd,[40] which was feued at £45 p.a.

One direct effect of the decrease in numbers joining the Trade was that fewer demands were made on the poor fund. In 1838 a general meeting of the Trade decided to divide the surplus of £260 among existing members or their heirs, and each received £10 at Lammas. Other Trades divided their funds rather later. In these circumstances it is a little odd to find that at the same time the entry fee was increased to £60 for strangers, £40 for sons-in-law and £20 for sons.[41] An annual division of funds, sometimes openly called a dividend, continued until 1961 though there were occasional breaks. In 1874, a Mr James Wanless, a member who had emigrated to Canada, was paid £47.10s.0d. to make up for the 32 years in which he had not received any money from the Trade.[42] After the handing out of that amount there was nothing for the rest of the Trade.

Members were not always happy about such distribution. In June 1854 the actual legality of the process was questioned, but the majority opinion was that consulting a lawyer was unnecessary.[43] When Mr Wanless made further claims on the Trade some years later on behalf of his widowed mother, as her husband had also been a member, demanding her share of all divisions of funds made since 1861, this action raised practical as well as legal and possibly moral issues.[44] When one hears of another widow being paid £30 in 1887 as arrears for her share, the implications for the Trade's funds could have been serious.[45]

Once again the legality of the division was considered, this time as to whether it was right to pay to members whose business lay outside the burgh bounds. A committee of the Trade decided this procedure was in order, one member Charles Ower dissenting. Mrs Wanless was offered £40 but nothing was heard from her until she applied to be entered on the Poor Roll in September 1890. This application was agreed as she was 75 years old.

In 1898 a new question arose concerning their funds which confirmed the uneasiness of at least some members of the incorporation about the annual division. There was some thought of selling the property in their possession which produced an income of £60. They meant to make provision for a poor fund and then to divide the proceeds among existing members. At that time there were fourteen members and only two pensioners, and for some time only sons or sons-in-law of freemasters had applied for entrance. Fortunately they took counsel from an Edinburgh lawyer, Mr John R. Baxter. His judgement was unequivocal. They held property in trust for themselves and future members; incorporations could not dissolve themselves but needed to apply to the Court of Session and further, he considered that the decision of 1838 to divide the surplus funds among members was illegal.[46]

The last part of his opinion they simply ignored but income from feu duties for property is still part of the Trade's income. In the more affluent

1950s members once again showed some doubts about receiving surplus funds, not so much legal as moral, and in 1959 it was suggested that money should be given to some small charities. This policy was agreed and thereafter organisations like the Old People's Welfare received contributions. In 1961 members were enjoined to give their dividend, the last in this century, to charity.

In its earlier days, the Weaver Trade attracted a large number of members. As we saw there were 119 members alive in 1761, and another 176 joined between that date and 1820. It must be assumed that some deacons were more enthusiastic about enrolling new members for there was not a regular flow of entrants. As factory and machine production gradually took over from home and hand crafts in the textile industry, the market for hand weaving decreased. This decline was reflected in the numbers who joined the Dundee Trade. By the middle of the nineteenth century entrants had decreased rapidly in numbers from the 119 recorded in 1761 – with a resultant drop in income.

After 1820 the entry of new numbers decreased even faster; from 1820 to 1846 there were only 18, none at all until 1852 and only 34 more by 1919, the Fairweather family making up a large proportion. In these circumstances the provision of a chain and badge for the Trade in 1882 seems slightly surprising.[47] Between 1919 and 1934 there was again a gap in recruitment and meetings were attended by only three or four of the Trade. From 1934 to 1980 only 23 more names appear in the Lockit Book; it was not surprising that concern about the society's numbers was expressed. However, while the Trade wanted new members, there was a reluctance to take 'positive action' to change its status from a closed to an open society.[48] It was felt that the textile industry in the town was still large enough to have potential members of the Weaver Trade.

The Trade has not always been so determined to retain its connection exclusively with the weaving trade. It may interest members to know that in the past, quite apart from honorary members, not all their predecessors were weavers. Lawyers, at least seven bankers between 1812 and 1821, a stationer, and a monumental sculptor all appear in the Lockit Books. In the early nineteenth century many new masters were described simply as manufacturers, but considering Dundee's economy at the time it is likely if not certain that they were textile manufacturers. For a few years after 1959 the occupation of some new entrants was given simply as 'gentleman'.

Of course, it is recognised that the change in the size of the incorporation in part reflects change in Dundee's industrial situation. While some textile

167

and associated industries still thrive in the town, they are no longer predominant. However, since 1980 over 40 new masters have been entered in the Lockit Book, all connected in some way with various branches of the textile industry, the clerks excepted. The Weaver Trade so far is succeeding in retaining its historical roots.

NOTES

[1] Quoted by Maxwell, 1891, 327.

[2] APS. ii. 376.

[3] Maxwell, 1884, 50–51; DDARC, GD/TD/W7.62.

[4] DDARC, GD/TD/W6.2, p. 61; W7.40; W9.4,5.

[5] DDARC, GD/TD/W7.9.

[6] DDARC, GD/TD/W7.1.

[7] DDARC, GD/TD/W6.2, p. 12; W7.2.

[8] DDARC, GD/TD/W7.9.

[9] NT5.2.1; Register of the Great Seal, 1513–1546 (1883) no. 996.

[10] DDARC, GD/TD/W6.7.

[11] DDARC, GD/TD/W6.2, pp. 10, 11.

[12] DDARC, GD/TD/W6.2, p. 14; 7.11.

[13] DDARC, GD/TD/W2.2, 4.5.1830.

[14] Ibid., 2.3.1836; 19.3.1841.

[15] DDARC, GD/TD/W2.1, 9.10.1759.

[16] DDARC, GD/TD/W1/1,2.

[17] DDARC, GD/TD/W1.2.

[18] DDARC, GD/TD/W1.1.

[19] DDARC, GD/TD/W1.3.

[20] DDARC, GD/TD/W3.1, 1763–64.

[21] DDARC, GD/TD/W2.1.

[22] DDARC, GD/TD/W6.2, p. 29, W7.17.

[23] DDARC, GD/TD/W7.19.

[24] DDARC, GD/TD/W1.1.

[25] DDARC, GD/TD/W7.23,29.

[26] DDARC, GD/TD/W6.2, p. 50.

[27] DDARC, GD/TD/W7.20.

[28] DDARC, GD/TD/W9.15.

[29] DDARC, GD/TD/W13.12.

[30] DDARC, GD/TD/W7.36.

[31] DDARC, GD/TD/W9.2.

[32] DDARC, GD/TD/W1.2.

[33] Warden, 1872, 529.

[34] Ibid., 536.

[35] DDARC, GD/TD/W8.5.

[36] DDARC, GD/TD/W1.1. I have not been able to identify 'boges'.

[37] DDARC, GD/TD/W2.2, 14.10.1825, 13.2.1832. Dates only are cited 37–40 as all are to be found in W2.2.

[38] 2.3.1835.

[39] 1836.

[40] 10.2.1824.

[41] 4.6.1838; 5.6.1838.

[42] WAB, in the care of the clerk.

[43] DDARC, GD/TD/W2.2, June 1854.

[44] DDARC, GD/TD/W2.3, 23.7.1886.

[45] Ibid., 9.6.1887.

[46] DDARC, GD/TD/W18.22.

[47] DDARC, GD/TD/W19.2.

[48] DDARC, GD/TD/W2.2, 5.11.1980.

CHAPTER 12

The United Trades of Dyers and Waulkers

It was 1693 before the Dyers, in Scots the Litsters, became full members of the Nine Trades, by means of a union formed with the Waulkers, the fullers of cloth, who had a much longer history as an incorporation and as a recognised constituent of the Nine. Neither was ever a large body in the town. Until the eighteenth century poorer Scots, the great majority in both town and country, wore garments of rough white or grey cloth which was neither dyed nor fulled. Sumptuary laws dictated how the various classes should be dressed, only whores being allowed to dress above their station. As a result, there was not an overwhelming demand for the finer materials which needed the skills of the litster or the waulker.

Though both crafts were involved in the finishing of cloth, the relations between them were poor at times, as we shall see. By uniting they formed a rather stronger body but despite the changes in fashion in the years after their union and the importance of textiles in Dundee's economy, their numbers have never been large and indeed, they have faced extinction at several times in their united history. Maintaining the tradition of a closed craft, they have today very few members.

The accepted name of the united Trade is now that of the younger society, though the new constitution of the Nine Trades gives both names. The history of the Dyers before 1693 will therefore be examined first. The Trade was not officially recognised by the town council as an organised Trade until 27 April 1590, when an Act of council was passed to that effect and ratified on 5 April 1619. A.J. Warden examined a copy of the second act when he was preparing *The Burgh Laws*. Unfortunately, only the Lockit Book, now with the name of the Dyers on its cover but originally the Waulker Trade's, was available for the purposes of this study.

At the end of the sixteenth century, after the Reformation, the Dyer Trade did not of course give the town council an undertaking to maintain an altar to a saint. In the text quoted by Warden[1] not even comparable duties are imposed on the Craft such as contributing to the parish ministers' stipends. But the Dyers were granted somewhat restricted privileges. On the one hand, it was decreed that no-one was to 'use the Litster Craft' except burgesses and freemen and those trained as apprentice under a skilful master. On the other, 'blaksteris', who used bark to produce black dye were allowed to continue this practice.

An even greater apparent threat to the Dyers' privileges was that merchants and guild brothers were allowed to set up their own vats, dye in any true colours they liked and employ anyone they liked to carry out these processes. The only restriction on them was that they must not dye goods belonging to those who were not burgesses or freemen of the burgh. Bonnet-makers too retained their power to dye their own materials. Not much monopoly seems to have been left here to the Dyer Craft itself and it is not perhaps surprising that the Trade's numbers remained small.

The reason for the re-enactment of the 1590 act in 1619 appears to have been the breach of two important clauses. Not all those empowered to practise litting (dyeing) had used the proper methods so that they were producing 'false and untrue' colours; perhaps worse, they had been dyeing not just for Dundee burgesses but for strangers from outside the town. In the later act the officers and sergeants of the burgh were instructed to obey any order from the magistrates to assist masters and freemen of the Trade to detain offenders in prison. This was a very powerful weapon in the Dyers' hands.

The Dyers must have thought that was quite an improvement in their status but, as was usual with many such laws, infringements continued and the act had to be repeated in 1643. Then fines of £5 were imposed for the first offence and doubled for each thereafter. In 1683, the Visitor, sometimes the name given to deacons for historical reasons, of the Litsters petitioned specifically against one offender, John Duncan, from the Hill of Dundee. According to this petition Duncan was a particularly bad case, having served no apprenticeship but he 'bragged' that he was a member of the Dundee Litster Trade. Worse, he produced very inferior work which was attributed to the Trade to the detriment of their reputation. Indeed, it would seem that some local craftsmen had been stoned by annoyed customers.[2]

One must wonder if any other than a Hill man would have been the object of such a diatribe but he was not the only sinner. The town councillors were sufficiently impressed to renew the powers of the Dyers to have such offenders imprisoned, under licence from the magistrates.

It is interesting that such draconian powers were granted to the Trade at this time, for in the past there had been some discrimination against dyers.

Under the Burgh Laws, the original rules which organised burgh society in Scotland, no dyer (or shoemaker or butcher) could become a member of the Merchant Guild unless he refrained from actively practising his trade, only employing servants to do the work.[3] It is believed that this was because of the apparent lack of cleanliness of dyers and these other tradesmen, as their hands were often almost indelibly stained through the nature of their work. In the fifteenth century dyers had also been restricted to dyeing goods belonging to others. In addition they could not buy cloth to dye and sell it on their own behalf.[4] Like weavers, dyers and waulkers were viewed with some suspicion by both burgh and central government; they too had to have the cloth they dealt with sealed to ensure its quality.[5]

During the seventeenth century the Dyer Trade remained small in number. Their relations with the Waulker Trade are the most important part of their history at the time as far as can be seen from the available records. It is perhaps therefore appropriate now to consider their partner-to-be, the Waulker Trade, the fullers of cloth.

The Waulker Trade, though last in precedence among the Nine, had become an incorporated Trade just as early as the other eight who now constitute the Nine. Their original charters were apparently seen by Warden but all we have now apart from the Lockit Book is a copy of King James V's ratification on 26 March 1527 of several charters and sasines and of their Seal of Cause. This copy is to be found among the Nine Trades records.[6]

The Waulkers had obtained endorsement by the town council on 12 September 1525, when James Scrymgeour was provost and constable and John Thomson was deacon of the Craft. The Craft undertook to repair an altar in the kirk in honour of Saint Mark, which was to be 'biggit (built) and repaired'. This may mean that they are simply taking over an existing altar situated west of the altar to St Michael and in front of a pillar next to it, but as bigging means building, they were perhaps constructing a new one. The usual conditions were offered regarding its upkeep and the payment of a chaplain. Masters were to pay one penny weekly and servants a half-penny; a freeman's son becoming master and setting up his booth to open his business would pay a pound of wax to the altar while others would pay 40s. Any strangers coming into the burgh to practise the trade were also due the same fees.

One clause in the Seal of Cause arose from a specific part of the waulkers' craft. Webs were often taken to waulk mills outside the town. If Dundee waulkers renting mills from landlords outside the town had any trouble with customers which needed recourse to courts of law, they were enjoined

171

that they must come first to the 'jurisdiction of the gude town'. They must not use their landlord's court, managed by his baron bailie, which was the usual place for settling disputes regarding tenants. The fine for breaking this rule was five merks and a stone of wax, half to St Mark's altar, half to the kirk. Unfortunately, with the lack of records, we cannot tell whether this clause was ever used or with what effect. It is unlikely that the removal of cases from their jurisdiction with the resulting loss of any fines imposed would be viewed with complaisance by lairds and heritors outside the burgh. The town council on the other hand had a vested interest in ensuring that cases were held in the burgh courts where they would benefit from any fines due.

The deacon's authority was upheld by the Seal of Cause, and the date of his election was fixed for the Sunday before St Mark's day, only freemen being allowed to vote. Other rules were similar to those of other Trades. Masters were to take only one apprentice at a time, a rule that seems to have been enforced. At one point even the death of the apprentice during the period of his indentures, five or six years, did not allow a master to begin training another. Admittedly this was during hard times, 1694, and its sheer impracticality must have led to its being rescinded a few years later.[7]

There was also a clause restricting prices for waulking cloth to what they had been in the past. Such an attitude would not have been popular in the middle of the next century. On 16 November 1669 the Trade talks with concern of inflation; they reckoned that in 'days of old' a small sum would have bought twenty times as much as it would at that date. Entry into the Trade was to be cut down to prevent a 'multitude' coming upon the Craft. Apprentice fees were duly raised to ten merks Scots and £40 Scots and a free dinner for the Trade – or another ten merks. Talk of a 'multitude' has to be looked at in perspective, when only ten members signed a statute in 1669 and there were only five waulkers in the incorporation when the Trade united with the Litsters in 1693.

In December 1582 the Waulker Trade passed or at least recorded on that date a whole string of statutes in their Lockit Book. Most of them were similar in nature to those of the other Crafts, regulating the terms of apprentices' indentures and time of service, discipline within the Craft, etc. Some of course referred to particular parts of the waulkers' craft; a sort of queueing system was laid down for using the mills on the Dichty, for instance, the first cloths that had been soaked (wetted) were to be the first fulled in the mills. Feeing of servants was to take place on only two days in the year, St Thomas' Day or Yule. A later statute undated, but earlier than

1671 as it was then confirmed and strengthened, forbade masters to look for work; they had to wait until a customer approached them.

In August 1671 the Trade deplored the deception used by some of their members in breaking this last rule. They had been employing other people, perhaps their wives and children, to ask for webs to dress, 'to the manifest prejudice of their brother Craftsmen who had formerly wrought to the said persons, against all law and reason and the good of comonweill'. Over and above the price of the piece of cloth obtained unfairly, as the Trade saw it, a fine of £10 was imposed for the future.

There was yet another practice which could have given an advantage to one master over his brethren, had it not met with the corporate disapproval of the Trade. On 6 May 1668 any master who made a yearly agreement with mill masters on the Dichty to treat his cloth for a fixed sum was fined £1. To modern eyes both this rule and that in the previous paragraph smack of restrictive practices, but competition among members was clearly frowned on. These rules illustrate the ethos of unity and cooperation which was a vital part of the incorporated Trades' philosophy.

The 1693 union of the Waulkers and the Litsters was not a forgone conclusion earlier in the century. Relations between the two were very bad only 24 years before. On 14 September 1669 the Waulkers declared that neither they nor their successors would accept any professing the litster or dyeing craft as a free waulker. Expulsion from the Trade would follow. Ten signed showing their agreement then, and eight years later on 15 October 1677 another five added their names.

A few years after the first adherence to the idea of keeping the other Craft at arms length, prices were fixed for waulking cloth for dyers on 26 October 1672. The prices seem high. Four shillings per ell for waulking and dressing broad cloth but no comparable figures appear in the Lockit Book for work done for other customers. The Trade expected that any infringements would be reported for the 'challenger or informant' had to prove the truth of his claim.

Despite such evidence of unfriendly feeling, only two decades later on 2 May 1693 the two Crafts signed a contract by which they became one. With only the Lockit Book to refer to, only surmise as to the reason for the change of heart is possible. It is not unlikely that the very small number of Waulkers had begun to feel that any increase in numbers and presumably resources arising from any such union would enable them to strengthen their position, particularly among the Nine Trades where they ranked as ninth and last. It is difficult to see what sort of case for change could have been made by the Waulkers without the union when it could be said, three years later in June 1696, that there were few members now living of the Waulker Trade 'who can dulie officiat the said calling'.[8] If such was their aim, however, it did not have any effect.

Amalgamation of the two incorporations was not a simple matter, either practically or legally. A charter from the monarch was required as well as ratification by parliament. William and Mary granted the charter under the Great Seal of Scotland on 28 February 1694 and the Three Estates ratified the charter on 17 July 1695.[9] When the Waulkers arranged for the admission of the ten existing dyers three weeks after the contract was signed, they had made the point that this reception could not take effect before parliamentary ratification of the union.[10] But at the same time, they did revoke the act of September 1669 which forbade the enrolment of litsters in the Trade. The united Trade also began to act as one before formal ratification. Various statutes in 1694 include regulations about dyeing as well as waulking.[11]

Whether the Dyer Trade has copies of any of these documents is unknown. The Weaver Trade, whose care of their records has been second to none, has retained a copy of the final agreement made in 1696, elaborating the conditions of the union, once all the legal matters had been decided.[12] The Waulkers had agreed to insert Litsters into their Lockit Book and this volume is still used by the Trade. All properly indentured apprentices from both Trades were to be accepted as free masters, though the Waulker Trade's privileges were to be maintained. The Litsters were also to accept waulkers as free litsters and both Trades were to train each other's children in their respective work, gratis.

For a limited period restrictions were retained on how much each could practise the other's craft. Waulkers recognised that with so few skilled in their trade, on the death of one or more of their number the 'lieges may be prejudiced'. Litsters did not apparently immediately begin to practise waulking. It was agreed in 1696 that they could dress cloth as long as they employed one qualified waulker approved by the Waulker deacon and boxmaster, James Mitchell and David Nicoll. Until both these men died, litsters were not to 'meddle' with cloth from Dundee, Fife nor the Carse. The existing waulkers, on their part, undertook not to trespass on the Dyer Trade's preserves.[13]

While the two Trades agreed to teach each other's offspring, the position of descendants might not have been sufficiently well clarified or perhaps even mentioned in the original contract. In August 1705 some of the waulkers brought this matter up. Being in a minority in the united incorporation they may have been more conscious of possible disadvantages.

The decision was recorded in the Lockit Book that none of their children should be excluded from both Trades any more than children of dyers.

During the last years of the seventeenth century the two groups were still very conscious of their separate natures, and rules were made in the name of both, though they seemed to refer mostly to dyeing. For instance, dyers seem to have sometimes paid their servants indirectly, by allowing them to dye pieces of cloth and take the money; this was a 'staig'. The length of cloth allowed was first restricted in 1694 and then the practice was totally prohibited in 1697. Understandably, at the later date, when the Scottish economy was in a very bad state, masters were not happy to have work taken out of their hands by their own workmen.

The union of the two small Trades was not welcomed at the time by either the Guildry or the Nine Trades. Again we must thank the Weavers for keeping a copy of the protestation made to parliament against the union.[14] This was recorded on the day that the Three Estates did in fact ratify their contract. The Guildry of Dundee, of which it was said the Litsters had 'ever been a member', were worried that their privileges might be affected, perhaps by an influx of waulkers. The Nine Trades were also worried as Dyers were not constitutionally part of their organisation; this was one reason for the united incorporation's keeping the Waulker name for a long time despite the smaller number in that Trade. The Nine Trades expressed special concern about the bonnetmakers' need to do their own dyeing. However the protest was perhaps a bit halfhearted and did not prevent the union.

The union did not result in the united Trade's going from strength to strength as the craftsmen of the two might have hoped. By 1829 fewer than 60 men had been admitted, including a few honorary members and some who were not practising dyers or waulkers, though sons of freemen. The Trade retained the name of Waulker and it is not clear just when Dyer superseded Waulker, for the latter title was still being used in the mid-nineteenth century and survives today in the Nine Trades' 1979 constitution. The Lockit Book which was the Waulkers' has been rebound with the title of the Dyers', but at some unknown date.

No new dyers entered the Trade in the 1830s and the situation arose that only one member survived, John Chapman, who had become a freemaster on 16 May 1823. Mr Chapman joined a meeting of the General Fund Court on 4 November 1839 and produced a minute of a meeting of the Waulker, not the Dyer, Trade of 22 July of that year, properly witnessed by two writers. At this meeting he had nominated himself deacon and boxmaster so that he could carry on his Trade's business.[15] He insisted on his right to sit on the General Fund Court but did at least leave the meeting while the matter was being discussed.

This was an unusual situation to say the least, and a decision was delayed until an adjourned meeting was held. Eventually a compromise was reached by which Mr Chapman was allowed to attend but a general meeting unanimously confirmed the decision of the General Fund Court that he should not be recognised as deacon or assessor.[16] If one member of the Nine Trades ceased to exist for all practical purposes because it had no members, there were legal implications for the town as a whole as well as for the Nine, which they were compelled to face. Representatives of the Nine as a corporate body had a legal position on the town council and on several boards which were vital in the town's administration, the Harbour Trust probably being the most important.

To avoid the possibility of any actions of such boards becoming invalid, the council and the Nine Trades applied to the Court of Session to appoint managers for the fairly moribund Waulker/Dyer incorporation. The managers were to attempt to resuscitate the Trade by admitting members and apprentices.[17] The Court duly agreed to this action and on 10 June 1840 named three managers, including John Chapman. The other two were the current deacon of the Bonnetmakers, Charles Fleming, and the Nine Trades convener, David Jobson.[18] Carrying out their instructions from the Lords of Council and Session, on 12 October that year the managers duly entered three new masters, all of them having dyeworks in Dundee. One, incidentally, was A.J. Warden.

The troubles of the Trade were not over. Mr Chapman for some reason took umbrage and raised objections to the entry of the three, on the grounds that they were not craftsmen. It should not be forgotten that he was one of the managers who had entered them in the first place. The matter was once again pursued before the Court of Session and the decision given on 19 March 1845. The end result was that these entries were deleted from the Lockit Book 'in terms of the minute of 15 May 1845', which must have discussed what action should follow the legal decision. Chapman had once again set himself up as deacon and in April 1845 admitted four masters, including John Stevenson, whose family dominated the Trade for the rest of the century.

Chapman at least had the satisfaction of having his election as deacon on 17 August 1833 declared in order by Lord Wood, the judge who heard the case. However, the whole episode was a costly one for the Trade, for the managers against whom Chapman raised the action were able to claim their costs out of the Trade's funds, and in the long run, the state of the

Trade did not improve. Though the Stevenson family were the backbone of the incorporation until the beginning of the twentieth century, even their interest seemed to fade after 1903. No new masters were entered in the Lockit Book from then until 1929 when two members' sons joined. From that date until 1970 when the last member was entered, only 22 have joined. Current members have attempted without success to enrol dyers in the town.[19] What a pity it will be if this small Trade does become extinct after four centuries.

NOTES

[1] Warden, 1872, 552–3.

[2] Ibid., 554.

[3] Grant, 1930, 135, 136.

[4] Warden, 1872, 540.

[5] Maxwell, 1884, 51, 52.

[6] NT5.2.1; *Register of the Great Seal* 1883 no. 435.

[7] DLB, 1.9.1694; 12.6.1697. In the care of the Trade.

[8] DDARC, GD/TD/W29.6.

[9] APS. ix. 131.

[10] DLB, 23.5.1693.

[11] DLB, 9.1.1694; 1.9.1694.

[12] DDARC, GD/TD/W29.6.

[13] DLB, 27.6.1696.

[14] DDARC, GD/TD/W29.5.

[15] NT2.7, 22.7.1839.

[16] NT2.6, 5.12.1839.

[17] Warden, 1872, 566.

[18] DLB.

[19] Information from Mr W. Philp; loose typed sheet within DLB dated 11.1.1982.

7. ANNUAL KIRKING OF THE NINE AND THE THREE UNITED TRADES, OCTOBER 1990

(The *Courier*, Dundee)

CHAPTER 13

Conclusion

By the end of the twentieth and the beginning of the twenty-first centuries the nine incorporated trades who are the constituent members of their society, The Nine Trades of Dundee, will have been in existence for almost 500 years. The craft that one Trade practised, bonnetmaking, is extinct as are some of the branches of the Hammermen Trade, such as gunmaking. The others can still be found in Dundee in varying degrees of prosperity.

The same can be said of the incorporations themselves. In 1981 there were 652 craftsmen, according to a count made by the Nine Trades. It is perhaps significant that the Bonnetmaker Trade which became an open Trade, in effect a social club, over 160 years ago in order to survive, was the largest in number at that date with 305 members. Next in size came the Bakers; 123 was their count, followed by 105 Fleshers, 90 Hammermen, 46 Tailors, 43 Cordiners, 23 Weavers, 20 Dyers and 17 Glovers, though the Tailors' numbers do not quite tally with their calculations.

All these men are automatically members of the Nine Trades which makes that society numerically strong, but without the Trades, the Nine could not exist as it does not enrol members except masters of the nine incorporations.

With the loss of their special privileges in 1846, individual Trades lost the mainspring of their existence. The provision of charity for poorer brethren, widows and orphans continues, in theory at least, even today and has no doubt been one factor in the continuing existence of the incorporations. However, it is unlikely that charitable purposes alone would have breathed as much life into potentially moribund societies as several of them un-doubtedly experience today. The size of the present membership of the Trades must surely show that long-remembered historical ties, interest in the past of the town and present pride of Dundee craftsmen in their trades are important factors that cannot be discounted.

In addition, there can be no doubt that the continuing existence of histor-ical societies like these, with their ancient traditions, artefacts and ceremon-ies, brighten the present and serve as a welcome reminder of our past.

INDEX